How to Study the Bible

VOLUME TWO

how to Study the Bible

OLIN T. BINKLEY

Mavis Allen, Editor

Convention Press
Nashville, Tennessee

This book is the text for course 3202 of the subject area Bible Studies of the Church
Study Course.
   Target group: This book is designed for adults and is part of the Church Study
Course offerings. The 1963 statement of ''The Baptist Faith and Message'' is the
doctrinal guideline for the writer and editor.

Dewey Decimal Classification Number: 220.07
Printed in the United States of America

Preface

You have just opened a first-of-its-kind book. HOW TO STUDY THE BIBLE is a manual for the person who desires to develop a good and consistent plan of Bible study. Prepared by Olin T. Binkley, former president of Southeastern Baptist Theological Seminary, this book is meant to inspire Bible study and to give guidelines for fruitful study.

This second volume in the Bible Survey series is composed of five basic chapters for study written by Dr. Binkley. Following chapters 2 through 5 there are articles to amplify and exemplify guidelines set forth by Dr. Binkley. Most of these articles contain helps for engaging in Bible study. It would be possible for a person or a group to take a Bible and this textbook and engage in study of the following books or portions of Scripture: 2 Kings 9–11; Psalm 116; Acts 10; Matthew 25; Daniel; Revelation; Habakkuk; John 2:1–11; 2 Corinthians; Romans, the Sermon on the Mount, and Ephesians. There are also suggestions for studying the central themes and important words of the Bible.

This book also contains two reading plans and charts for recording progress on the plans, a chart of the English Bible, a sample of the author's suggestion for keeping a notebook on Bible reading. Other helpful articles are placed advantageously throughout the book. Of particular help to the person embarking on a lifetime of Bible study will be the annotated bibliography which may serve as a guide to building a library of Bible study tools.

In *An Introduction to the Bible* (vol. 1 in this series), L. D. Johnson challenged his readers to seek a deeper understanding of God's revelation to man. This book was prepared to help the Christian do just that. For a list of coming volumes in the series, see the back cover of this book.

The Church Study Course

The Church Study Course consists of a variety of short-term credit courses for adults and youth and noncredit foundational units for children and pre-schoolers. The materials are for use in addition to the study and training curriculums made available to the churches on an ongoing basis.

Study courses and foundational units are organized into a system that is promoted by the Sunday School Board, 127 Ninth Avenue, North, Nashville, Tennessee 37234, through the departments in the Church Services and Materials Division; by the Woman's Missionary Union, 600 North Twentieth Street, Birmingham, Alabama 35203; by the Brotherhood Commission, 1548 Poplar Avenue, Memphis Tennessee 38104; and by the respective departments of the state conventions affiliated with the Southern Baptist Convention.

Study course materials are flexible enough to be adapted to the needs of any Baptist church. The resources are published in several different formats—textbooks of various sizes, workbooks, and kits. Each item contains a brief explanation of the Church Study Course and information on requesting credit. Additional information and interpretation are available from the participating agencies.

Types of Study and Credit

Adults and youth can earn study course credit through individual or group study. Teachers of courses or of foundational units also are eligible to receive credit.

1. Class Experience.—Group involvement with course material for the designated number of hours for the particular course. A person who is absent from one or more sessions must complete the "Personal Learning Activities" or other requirements for the course.
2. Individual Study.—This includes reading, viewing, or listening to course material and completing the specified requirements for the course.
3. Lesson Course Study.—Parallel use of designated study course material during the study of selected units in Church Program Organization periodical curriculum units. Guidance for this means of credit appears in the selected periodical.
4. Institutional Study.—Parallel use of designated study course material during regular courses at educational institutions, including Seminary Extension Department courses. Guidance for this means of credit is provided by the teacher.

Credit is awarded for the successful completion of a course of study. This credit is granted by the Church Study Course Awards Office, 127 Ninth Avenue, North, Nashville, Tennessee 37234, for the participating agencies. Form 151 (available free) is recommended for use in requesting credit.

When credit is issued to a person on request, the Awards Office sends two copies of a notice of credit earned to the church. The original copy of the credit slip should be filed by the study course clerk in the participant's record of training folder. The duplicate should be given to the person who earned the credit. Accumulated credits are applied toward leadership or member development diplomas, which are measures of learning, growth, development, and training.

Detailed information about the Church Study Course system of credits, diplomas, and record keeping is available from the participating agencies. Study course materials, supplementary teaching or learning aids, and forms for record keeping may be ordered from Baptist Book Stores.

The Church Study Course Curriculum
Credit is granted on those courses listed in the current copy of *Church Services and Materials Catalog*, *Church Study Course Catalog*, and *Baptist Book Store Catalog*. When selecting courses or foundational units, check the current catalogs to determine what study course materials are valid.

How to Request Credit for This Course

This book is the text for course 3202 of the subject area Bible Studies.

This course is designed for ten hours of group study. Credit is awarded for satisfactory class experience with the study material for the minimum number of hours. A person who is absent from one or more sessions must complete the "Personal Learning Activities" or other requirements for the materials missed.

Credit is also allowed for use of this material in individual study and in institutional study, if so designated.

The following requirements must be met for credit in course 3202:
1. Read the book *How to Study the Bible*.
2. Attend at least ten hours of class study or complete all "Personal Learning Activities" (pp. 177-78). A class member who is absent from one or more class sessions must complete "Personal Learning Activities" on chapters missed. In such a case, he must turn in his paper by the date the teacher sets, usually within ten days following the last class.

Credit in course 3202 may be earned through individual study. The requirements for such credit are:
1. Read the book.
2. Complete the "Personal Learning Activities" on the chapters.

Credit in course 3202 may be earned through study in an educational institution, if so designated by a teacher. The requirements are:
1. Read the book.
2. Fulfill the requirements of the course taught at the institution.

After the course is completed, the teacher, the study course records librarian, the learner, or any person designated by the church should complete Form 151 ("Request for Course Credit, Revised 1975") and send it to the Awards Office, 127 Ninth Avenue, North, Nashville, Tennessee 37234. In the back of this book the reader will find a form which he may cut out, fill in, and send to the Awards Office.

Contributors: Robert A. Baker; D. P. Brooks; A. Stuart Arnold; B. A. Sizemore; Kenneth Wolfe; Roy Honeycutt; George Thomason; Morris Ashcraft; Richard Kornmeyer; Ralph McLain; Edgar McKnight; Robert A. Dean; and Charles F. Treadway.

Contents

CHAPTER ONE

Why Study
the Bible
Today

The very fact that you have taken this book into your hands to read it—either in preparation for a class session or for your own personal study at home—is clear indication that you are aware of the importance of Bible study. No doubt you have taken seriously the injunction of 2 Timothy 2:15: "Do your best to present yourself to God an approved workman who has nothing to be ashamed of, who properly presents the message of truth" (Williams).[1]

One Christian educator has raised this question: "How could one adopt and develop a Christian way of life without making the Bible his own, without seeking through all the days and years of his life to understand it, appreciate it, and come to the place where its truth and teachings are the very focus of his living?" [2]

The purpose of this book is to present guidelines for a serious and sincere study of the Bible. It is addressed to those persons who desire to read the Bible with understanding and to relate its message to the decisions and duties confronting the people of God in this decisive age. It draws attention to the available resources and fruitful methods of Bible study which have been discovered in the writings of biblical scholars, in conversations with pastors and teachers, and through personal experience.

---

[1] Charles B. Williams, *The New Testament in the Language of the People* (Chicago: Moody Press, 1955).
[2] D. Campbell Wyckoff, *The Task of Christian Education* (Philadelphia: The Westminster Press, 1955), p. 67.

Systematic and thorough study is essential if one is to hear accurately and interpret responsibly what God is saying through the Bible. A rapid reading of large sections of the Bible is valuable, but it is only a preparation for intensive and unhurried study of the moral and spiritual message set forth in the words, books, and central themes of God's revelation. Such study requires intellectual integrity, appropriate methods, and persistent work.

Inasmuch as the context in which any study is conducted becomes a part of the learning process, the context of Bible study deserves careful consideration. In contemporary American culture, four contexts or situations appear to be favorable for a thorough study of the Scriptures: (1) *a home in which religious faith is a vital force in daily living and in which parents teach children how to study the Bible effectively;* (2) *a church which uses the educational method in the fulfilment of its mission and places high value upon Bible study;* (3) *a Bible study group composed of persons committed to the search for truth, the struggle for justice, and the ministry of reconciliation;* (4) *a college, university, or theological seminary in which professors and students carry on biblical research, including linguistic, literary, historical, and theological studies.* The methods of Bible study recommended in this book are related primarily to the home and the church, but they also involve materials produced by competent and devout scholars in seminaries and universities.

The human family has grown enormously in recent decades, but only a minority of its members manifest any personal interest in the Bible. For this reason, though you probably would not be reading this book if you were not concerned about Bible study, we examine candidly the question, Why study the Bible today?

Before we come to grips with this straightforward question, two preliminary considerations merit recognition: Let us be reminded first that competent biblical scholars have written books to enable thoughtful men and women, including those who are not proficient in the use of Hebrew and Greek, to achieve a trustworthy understanding of the major aspects of biblical thought. A brief, but adequate, list of these scholarly works will be discussed in the next chapter. We should remember also that God is speaking to us through the Bible. This collection of sixty-six books is an inexhaustible source of light and power for us as we look at the imperative tasks confronting us in our homes, in our work, and as we take our places where decisions are made. If we examine carefully all that is said in the Bible, we shall be able to think and speak honestly and wisely about God, about ourselves, about our neighbors, about what is going on in our day, and about what we ought to do now.

There is ample evidence that whenever sincere and intelligent persons come together to search for effective ways to meet human need and participate in serious study of the Bible they find guidance and strength. This was true in England during World War II when lonely people met together, contrary to instructions from governmental authorities because of the air raids, and formed Bible study groups. They formed friendships at deep levels of understanding and appreciation. In Germany after World War II, many farmers had food in their barns while people in large cities were hungry. Some of these farmers met in small groups for Bible study to discover what they ought to do.[3] Truth and guidance from the Bible are found today when small groups of fathers and mothers come together to think about the need for Christian environment in which to teach their children. They turn to the Bible with teachable minds and wistful hearts to find ways to make good communities better.

The following analysis of incentives for Bible study today is based primarily upon the nature and purpose of the Scriptures. It also takes into account the relevance of the biblical message to the questions of the human mind and to the distresses of the human heart in contemporary culture. Why are enlightened persons encouraged to study the Bible in a technological society?

TO RECLAIM A RELIGIOUS HERITAGE

A thorough study of the Bible will enable us to retrieve valuable elements of our heritage.

Bible study will remind us that God is the ultimate source of all resources, that he is the Creator of the universe and man, that he is creatively and redemptively at work in the church and in the world, and that freedom and authority are derived from him.

Bible study will bring before our eyes the primary documents of the history and religion of Israel and the earliest Christian churches. If the Bible had never been written, or if it had been destroyed beyond recovery, it would be extremely difficult to reconstruct the

---

[3] E. H. Robertson, *Take and Read* (London: SCM Press, 1961), pp. 44, 16.

history of Israel in its most creative periods or to understand the
origin of Christianity.

Bible study will permit us to discover and follow the principles
of Christian behavior undergirded by Christian faith in our search for
a clear understanding of life. This is an exceptionally important and
difficult task and should be given higher priority than it has received
in American homes and churches.

TO GAIN KNOWLEDGE OF GOD

A careful and conscientious study of the Bible increases our
knowledge of God and his redemptive purpose. It permits us to see
and hear what the writers of the Bible saw and heard, and to interpret
the meaning of biblical events in the perspective of God's righteous
rule in the affairs of men.

In an effort to understand the message of the Bible and its
relation to what we think and do in the communities in which we live,
it is important for us to remember four things about man's knowledge
of God.

**Our knowledge of God comes to us through an understanding of his
self-revelation throughout history.**

One of the ways he has revealed himself is through his mighty
acts in the history of the Hebrew people. He called Abraham and
promised to establish a community which would be a channel of
blessing to all the families on earth (Gen. 12:1–3). God delivered his
people from bondage in Egypt. This deliverance was interpreted as a
manifestation of his power in the fulfilment of a promise. He said:
" 'I have seen the affliction of my people who are in Egypt, and have
heard their cry because of their taskmasters; I know their sufferings,
and I have come down to deliver them out of the hand of the
Egyptians, and to bring them up out of that land to a good and broad
land' " (Ex. 3:7–8, RSV).

God entered into a covenant with his people and promised them
a land in which to live. The requirements and the promises of the
covenant became a part of the memories recorded in the Old Testament. " 'I call heaven and earth to witness against you this day, that I
have set before you life and death, blessing and curse; therefore
choose life, that you and your descendants may live, loving the Lord
your God, obeying his voice, and cleaving to him; for that means life
to you and length of days, that you may dwell in the land which the

Lord swore to your fathers, to Abraham, to Isaac, and to Jacob, to give them'" (Deut. 30:19–20, RSV). God spoke to his people through the prophets who heard the voice of God and then declared the message with clarity and courage. Jeremiah, for example, understood his task as an interpreter of God's will: "But the Lord said to me, 'Do not say, "I am only a youth"; for to all to whom I send you you shall go, and whatever I command you you shall speak'" (Jer. 1:7, RSV).

Our knowledge of God comes through Jesus Christ.

Christ is the perfect revelation of God's character and purpose. The New Testament announces the good news that the living God, who spoke through the Law and the Prophets, acted decisively for man's redemption in the life, death, and resurrection of Jesus Christ. Paul said in his message to the Christians at Corinth, "For God, who commanded the light to shine out of darkness, hath shined in our hearts, to give the light of the knowledge of the glory of God in the face of Jesus Christ" (2 Cor. 4:6).

In the fulness of time, the mind of God was disclosed through a man who was full of grace and truth. The author of Hebrews wrote: "In many and various ways God spoke of old to our fathers by the prophets; but in these last days he has spoken to us by a Son, whom he appointed the heir of all things, through whom also he created the world" (Heb. 1:1–2, RSV).

Our knowledge of God comes through obedience to his will.

We know God when we reverently acknowledge what he has done for the salvation of men, commit ourselves without reservation to our Lord and his way of life, and practice justice and brotherly kindness. We are reminded in John's Gospel that "if any man will do his will, he shall know of the doctrine, whether it be of God, or whether I speak of myself" (John 7:17).

The God of the Bible is not an abstraction or an idea to be known solely through an intellectual process of observation and contemplation. He is the God of Abraham, Isaac, and Jacob (Ex. 3:6). He is the God and Father of our Lord Jesus Christ. He has spoken to us through his mighty acts in the history of Israel and through his Son. His word is near to us, and we can respond to it (Deut. 30:14); and in obedient response to his word, we know him and love him with mind, heart, soul, and strength.

Our knowledge of God comes through the Bible.

The Bible records the events of history, and it interprets the meaning of the events. It speaks to men in every generation about what God has done for his people and what they ought to do as his children.

At this point, we face squarely some central issues regarding the value and relevance of the Bible. If all that has come to us from the Bible should be eliminated or forgotten, what would we know about the history and religion of Israel during the period covered by the Old Testament? What would we know of God's decisive action in the life, death, and resurrection of Jesus Christ? What would we know of the earliest disciples of Jesus? Would we know of the proclamation that God was in Christ reconciling the world unto himself? Would we know that he confronted men in a particular context of time and place and declared his claim upon them, that through Jesus he communicated the assurance that he knows men of faith as they are and loves them? The truth is that while secular history would tell us some of these things, our knowledge would be scant indeed apart from the Bible.

There are additional questions to be faced. Do we really want to know who God is and what he has done for his people? Are we seriously concerned about his purpose in history and its relation to what we do and say in this generation? Do we sincerely desire to know Jesus Christ and the implications of his words and deeds for the decisions we make? Are we eager to learn what the Bible teaches about the love of God and neighbor? If we answer these questions affirmatively, we can find a place in our schedules to read the Bible with scrupulous care and to reflect upon what we find in it.

TO ENCOUNTER THE CALL TO COMMITMENT

In a comprehensive and intensive study of the Bible we encounter Jesus Christ, in whom the authentic but unfulfilled message of the Old Testament was fulfilled. In our encounter with the Bible, we respond affirmatively or negatively to Christ's invitation to listen to him, to trust him, and to follow him. An affirmative response to an encounter with God is necessary for salvation and can be called Christian commitment.

Every person whose mind is exposed to the total message of the Bible sooner or later wrestles with the crucial question: What will you do with Jesus? What will you do with his revelation of God? What will you do with his interpretation of life? What will you do with his call to discipleship? What will you do with his moral directives? These are not superficial questions. They are to be pondered deeply. And in the privacy of the individual mind and heart, one says yes or no to Jesus Christ.

Who is the Christ?

The Christ whom we meet in the pages of the New Testament confronts us not in the faraway places and in the long ago, but right here and right now and he expects a decision from us. The question then is whether or not we are ready to make a personal commitment to the Christ made known to us in historical documents written by men. The Christ whom we confront in the Scriptures is the one through whom God communicated his grace and truth to men in Palestine in the first half of the first century of the Christian era. He is Christ whose love for men and identification with them brought him to a painful death on the cross. The Christ who calls us to commitment is the Christ whom God raised from the dead and who is alive forevermore. He is the pioneer of faith, the Saviour and Lord of those who are personally committed to him. To commit ourselves to such a Lord is not easy. But this is the challenge to decision presented to us through the Bible.

What are the implications of an affirmative response to the invitation of our Lord Jesus Christ?

The Christian decision involves a moral transformation of the individual and a sharpening of personal identity. Every dimension of man's life has been touched and hurt by sin, but when one opens his inner life to God in repentance, the Spirit of God penetrates to the roots of sin in his soul. The Holy Spirit produces a radical transformation, a new creation (2 Cor. 5:17). The redeemed one is re-created, renewed, reconciled, and given a fresh opportunity for the fulfilment of his personal potential.

The Christian decision involves acceptance of the gift of eternal life. The statement in the Gospel of John, " 'I came that they may have life, and have it abundantly' " (John 10:10, RSV), does not mean the intensification of the physical life which has been transmitted from parents to children. The life of which John wrote is the new life imparted to the believer through Christ. It is eternal life, the kind of life which is qualitatively worth living. It is the life which a man receives by the grace of God when he changes his mind and turns in a new direction. It was this quality of life that Paul spoke of when he said: "It is no longer I who live, but Christ who lives in me" (Gal. 2:20, RSV).

The Spirit of God draws redeemed men and women into the fellowship of the people of God. This is the process by which Christian communities are created. The Christian church is an institution with a history, a structure, a program, and a leadership. But a church is primarily a fellowship of believers who have responded affirmatively to God's call in Jesus Christ and have experienced a radical moral transformation. It is a fellowship in which Jesus Christ is acknowledged as Lord, the Bible is read and interpreted, men and women are not ashamed to pray, and each individual is treated as a person. It is the mission of the church to proclaim the gospel of the grace of God, to teach committed persons the Christian way of life, to stimulate and guide the growth of persons in Christian maturity, and to maintain a vital relation between the worship of God and participation in the needful work of the world. The local congregation, as one scholar has pointed out, may be regarded as the primary unit of the Christian fellowship in which neighbors strengthen one another in the faith, "correct one another in love," and "wait together on the Lord for his guidance." [4]

Christian commitment prepares men to deal intelligently with change. We are confronted daily with changes in our families, in our colleagues, in our communities, in international relations, and in the world economy. This places us under great strain and tests our capacity to anticipate change, to discern its direction, to estimate its rate, to evaluate its consequences, and, in some instances, to redirect it.

In order to understand and interpret change, we need to see it not only in historical and cultural perspectives but also in the light of the mind of Christ as presented in the Bible. It can be said of our Lord that he is the same yesterday, today, and forever. He gives us a fixed point outside ourselves by which to test change and find the right direction. An affirmative response to the invitation to Bible study helps us to find this direction.

---

[4] Lesslie Newbigin, *The Household of God* (New York: Friendship Press, 1954), p. 117.

PERSONAL VALUES OF BIBLE STUDY

We have explored three reasons for a thorough study of the Scriptures today: It will enable us to retrieve valuable elements of our heritage, enlarge and deepen our knowledge of God, and clarify the essence and implications of Christian commitment. It is appropriate now to consider four personal values of Bible study set forth by Paul in his letter to the Christians in Rome. He wrote: "Whatever was written in former days was written for our instruction, that by steadfastness and by the encouragement of the scriptures we might have hope" (Rom. 15:4, RSV).

In the Bible we have access to the most valuable instruction.

The Bible holds a message about God and man which speaks directly to our need to be accepted, to be forgiven, to be loved, and to be guided in the path of righteousness. The word "learning" and the word "instruction" have a twofold meaning.

Learning or instruction can refer to a body of knowledge. *The Oxford English Dictionary,* for example, is a large and refined body of knowledge. The Library of Congress at Washington, D. C., contains an enormous collection of books, a carefully organized body of knowledge to which creative thinkers and writers have contributed. The Bible, including the Old and New Testaments, is an inspired and unique body of learning. The Old Testament is related to the New by religious and moral as well as historical bonds, and these dynamic ties are never to be cut. The whole book is "profitable for teaching, for reproof, for correction, and for training in righteousness, that the man of God may be complete, equipped for every good work" (2 Tim. 3:16–17, RSV).

Learning or instruction is a process. It is a search for knowledge, a discovery of truth, a struggle for the mastery of ideas, an effort of the mind to see what is, what has been, and what ought to be. The Bible stimulates the love of learning and teaches us to use our minds in harmony with God's purpose.

The valuable instruction available in the Bible produces steadfastness in our lives.

This quality of Christian character was urgently needed by the Christians in the city of Rome to whom Paul wrote concerning the purpose and power of the Scriptures. It is urgently needed by God's people in the buildings and on the streets of American cities at this moment. It is needed in the church, in the schoolhouse, in the courthouse, and in the home.

The God whom we worship is the God of "steadfastness" (Rom. 15:5, RSV). He controls the creative power of the universe and relates it to the people who participate in the fulfilment of his purpose.

Steadfastness is the ability to suffer and be strong. It is the capacity to make a commitment and to be loyal to a cause in spite of the most adverse circumstances, including unrelenting cruelty and the peril of destruction. Steadfastness is inward strength to endure the outward pressures of responsible living. It is the willingness to get under a burden and to remain there, without falling down and without running away, to the end of the journey. It is characteristic of a tough-minded, tenderhearted man of faith, who has a clear vision of a purpose to be achieved and carries responsibility with faithfulness and courage.

We have watched enterprises in which men and women have drawn from the message of the Bible strength to bear heavy burdens. For example, consider the mayor of a large city who had a strong sense of justice and a concern for the well-being of all the people in a metropolitan area. He endured unmerciful criticism daily because he had a vision of a city with moral as well as legal foundations "whose builder and maker is God." We remember a woman who assumed responsibility for a business at the time of her husband's death and carried the duty for decades in spite of loneliness and illness. These persons, and countless others, have been steadfast in their reverence for God, in their loyalty to Jesus Christ, in their devotion to the church, and in their vocations. They were nurtured and nourished by the authentic and vital message of the Bible. A study of the Scriptures developed in them a steadfastness of Christian character.

The instruction of the Bible creates encouragement in us.

In the biblical message, "comfort" or "encouragement" is an attitude of mind derived from the assurance that God encourages his people by his presence in their midst and by what he has communicated to them through the Law, the Prophets, and Jesus Christ. This encouragement includes the understanding that in some real sense God goes with every person whom he sends forth on a mission to guide him, to sustain him, and to encourage him.

A thoughtful reading of the Bible enables servants of God to maintain a relatively high frustration level even in days of adversity. If the frustration level is low, it is easy for a person to lose heart, become discouraged, feel depressed, and forget available resources. If the frustration level is high, a person can maintain objectivity, evaluate situations intelligently, maintain personal integrity, and work without excessive mental anguish. The God of the Bible is the God of encouragement, and his message causes the believer to take new heart.

In a book entitled *Home Life in the Bible,* Emma Williams Gill recorded many insights into the relation of biblical faith and truth to the quality of life in the family. She had examined all references in the Bible to daily living in the home with special attention to the role of the wife and mother. She described ways in which mothers expressed the biblical attitude of encouragement to children in the homes she had visited in many lands. She told about a banquet at which the guests were speaking of their happiest memories of childhood. One guest, a former Secretary of Labor, was silent for a long time because he could think of no happy memories of his childhood. His family had felt the pinch of poverty, and after the father's death the two boys had worked in the mines. It was hard and dangerous work. But at last one happy memory came to his mind. It was the memory of his mother who kept hot tea ready for the boys and who always stood at the open door, held a lamp high in her hand, and sang as the boys went to work in the morning and as they returned from work at night. She was undergirded by faith in God and knew how to encourage children to face and overcome the difficulties of life.[5]

One of the objectives of an educational foundation for religious leaders in the United States is "to establish a relationship of encouragement" with persons to whom awards are made for graduate study. This objective appears to be in harmony with the purpose of God to create an attitude of encouragement to steadfastness in the minds of his people.

The message of the Bible keeps alive hope in our hearts.

In the purpose of God, the Bible was written for our instruction that, remaining steadfast and drawing encouragement from the divine revelation, we might have hope for the future.

---

[5] Emma Williams Gill, *Home Life in the Bible* (Nashville: Broadman Press, 1936), p. 188.

In the total message of the Bible, "hope" is a predominant theme. Hope is rooted and grounded in God, who makes promises to his people and is able to fulfil them. It is manifested in man's affirmative response to what God has done for his people and to what God has promised to those who love and serve him. Hope is vitally related to faith, love, freedom, boldness, and steadfast endurance (Rom. 5:4–5; 8:20; 1 Cor. 13:13; 2 Cor. 3:12). It is a strong anchor of the soul (Heb. 6:19).

We live in a mood of expectancy. We do not know what a day may bring forth, but we face the future with confidence and hope. This hope is not based upon who man is and what he can do, but upon the power and steadfast love of God who is the Lord of history and whose promises are recorded in the Bible.

We have learned that there is something of supreme worth for our lives in the Bible which is available nowhere else. We have witnessed an unprecedented expansion of knowledge during the past two decades. This advancement of learning is a product of the capabilities of the human mind and of the scientific method of research. It is to be received with gratitude, assimilated without fear, and utilized for the well-being of man. It is to be remembered, however, that this large and growing body of information neither displaces nor invalidates the unique message of the Bible. In many respects, the scientific revolution has intensified man's need of God's grace. For thoughtful men and women to ignore the Bible at this point in human history would be culturally inexcusable and spiritually disastrous. *A thorough study of the Bible will enable us to retrieve valuable elements of our spiritual heritage, to enter into a deeper knowledge of God, to respond affirmatively to the mission and message of Jesus Christ, and to participate in a collection and process of learning which will give steadfastness, encouragement, and hope.*

CHAPTER TWO

Resources
for
Bible Study

In history there is a spiritual leadership composed of men and women who have intellectual ability, moral integrity, vocational competence, and religious faith.

This kind of leadership is urgently needed in every dimension of American life at this moment. We are moving into a new era in which we are confronted daily with complex issues and excessive demands. In this dynamic situation we are required to make decisions concerning priorities.

In the quest for a coherent interpretation of life, one must be guided by honest and profound study of the Bible. In addition to scientific knowledge and technical skill, which are indispensable in a technological society, we seek a clear understanding of moral standards to guide our minds in hours of decision. We long for a deepening of the intellectual and spiritual life which springs from faith in God.

We have examined the values of Bible study. *In this chapter we are concerned with the question: What resources for a thorough study of the Bible in the English language are available to us?*

THE BIBLE IN ENGLISH

We have access to the Bible in the English language. This is a tremendous asset to be accepted with gratitude and to be used with integrity in the search for a Christian interpretation of life.

Although a knowledge of Greek, Hebrew, and Aramaic is desirable in the study of the Bible, we can explore the message of the Bible at great depth in the English language. We can now come to the Bible in English translations with the assurance that through the faithful work of biblical scholars we are dealing with the substance of the documents of the Christian faith.

A study of the Bible in English will be enhanced by attention to three subjects: the composition, collection, and selection of the books of the Bible; the search for an accurate and comprehensive text of the Bible; the history of the translation of the Bible into the English language. In keeping with the purpose of this book on how to study the Bible, we will refer briefly to the first two of these subjects and then focus attention upon several English versions of the Bible.

Process of Composition, Collection, and Selection

The composition, collection, and selection of the books of the Bible involved a long process. The message of God came through the minds of men under the inspiration of the Holy Spirit and was recorded in documents. The documents were read and appreciated by devout servants of God, gradually collected, and finally approved for inclusion in the Old or New Testament.

Although the growth of the Hebrew Bible, composed of three groups of books entitled the Law, the Prophets, and the Writings, extended over several centuries, the process can be traced with a reasonable degree of definiteness and was completed prior to A.D. 90. At that time the Council of Jamnia accepted this collection of books as the sacred and authoritative writings of the Jewish faith.

After careful deliberation, the early Christians accepted the four Gospels and twenty-three additional Christian documents, including the letters by Paul, to form the New Testament. The outcome of the process of usage and common consent by which the Christians selected the books of the New Testament was known by A.D. 367, at which time Athanasius in an Easter letter identified the twenty-seven books of the New Testament as we have them today.

Search for an Accurate Translation

The early Christians recognized the worth of the Old Testament and combined the two testaments to form one book. The search for an accurate and comprehensive text of the Bible, based upon the most careful examination of an enormous number of manuscripts, has made solid progress toward the recovery of the original work of the biblical writers. We do not possess any of the original manuscripts of the books of the Bible. We do not have, for example, the original manuscript of any book of the New Testament as it left the author's hand. The originals of both Testaments have long since disappeared; and in their place we have thousands of copies in Hebrew, Greek, and the various languages into which the Hebrew and Greek were translated. This is the reason many of the ablest biblical scholars have devoted their lives to a study of the text of the Old and New Testaments to determine insofar as possible precisely what the authors wrote. This scientific study of available manuscripts, including the Dead Sea scrolls, has not extended all the way back to the originals. However, it has provided a reproduction of the original work of the biblical writers which apparently approaches an accurate and comprehensive text of the Old and New Testaments.

The translation of the Bible from the languages in which it was originally written into the languages of the people who read it has been exacting in its demands. It has required the painstaking labor of a large number of biblical scholars who have worked to determine the best text of the Bible and to understand the changes in living languages. It has been a tedious and, in some instances, a very dangerous undertaking; but it has permitted the people of many lands and cultures to study the Bible in their own language.

The Old Testament was translated into Greek in Alexandria by the middle of the third century B.C. This oldest translation of the Old Testament into Greek, the work of seventy or seventy-two scholars, is known as the Septuagint. Commonly abbreviated LXX, this early translation has been influential throughout the history of Christianity. It was widely used as the Bible by the early Christians and was a vital factor in the production of the Old Latin versions and the subsequent daughter translations such as the Coptic, the Ethiopic, and the Armenian.

We should note, also, that Jerome, a distinguished biblical scholar, translated the Bible into Latin at a monastery in Bethlehem at the end of the fourth century. At first his version was severely criticized, but its value was later recognized. It was called the Vulgate, "the common version," and was used as the Bible throughout Western Christendom. It was from this version that the Bible was first translated into English.

History of English Translations

A study of the history of the translation of the Bible into English reveals, among other things, the hunger of a people for the Bible in their mother tongue and the competence and dedication of a long line of biblical scholars. Although the psalms and the Gospel of John were translated into Anglo-Saxon as early as the eighth century, the first translation of the entire Bible into English appeared about 1382 and was primarily the work of John Wycliffe. This translation was based on the Latin Vulgate and was the only complete English Bible in use for approximately one hundred and fifty years.

In this book we do not attempt to trace the long history of the translation of the Bible into English. Instead, we draw special attention to three English versions of the Bible which are exceptionally valuable to biblical students today. These are the King James Version, the American Standard Version, and the Revised Standard Version. The emphasis we place upon these versions is not intended to discourage the use of translations of the Bible by such biblical scholars as Moffatt, Goodspeed, Weymouth, Williams, Phillips, Bratcher, and others. (Some of these are discussed briefly in this chapter.) We advise the reading of recent translations of the Bible. At the same time, we recognize a meaningful continuity in the three versions we have selected for consideration. The preface to the Revised Standard Version explicitly states that it is "an authorized revision of the American Standard Version, published in 1901, which was a revision of the King James Version, published in 1611."

In January, 1604, King James approved a proposal by John Reynolds that a new translation of the Bible should be made. On February 10 of that year, the king ordered that a translation be made of the Bible "as consonant as can be to the original Hebrew and Greek"; [1] and on July 22, 1604, he announced that he had appointed fifty-four learned men to undertake the task. For the most part, these men were devout and able scholars and worked diligently and systematically for approximately six years. They were instructed to follow the Bishops' Bible with as little alteration "as the truth of the original will permit." [2]

---

[1] J. R. Branton, "English Versions," *The Interpreter's Dictionary of the Bible* (New York: Abingdon Press, 1962) IV, 766.

[2] S. L. Greenslade, "English Versions of the Bible, 1525–1611," *The Cambridge History of the Bible*, edited by S. L. Greenslade (New Rochelle, N. Y.: Cambridge University Press, 1963), p. 377.

It was the purpose of these scholars to produce a good translation characterized by accuracy and literary excellence. However, their work was hindered by limitations—the Hebrew and Greek texts available to them left much to be desired; their knowledge of Hebrew was imperfect; and the directives to be followed were restrictive.

Despite these limitations, however, they worked honestly and faithfully. Drawing upon the labors of earlier biblical scholars, they prepared a version which for more than three centuries has been the best known and most widely-used Bible in the English-speaking world. It was the judgment of B. F. Westcott that, after taking into account every "inconsistency of practice and inadequacy of method," the work of these scholars "issued in a version of the Bible better— because more faithful to the original—than any which had been given in English before." [3]

In spite of defects of varying sorts and import, it is to be said that the version of the Bible produced in 1611 revealed the solid results of biblical scholarship. It reflected a knowledge of the biblical languages and has made a strong appeal to the religious impulses of many Christian people. It released a vitality derived from the message it communicated and was capable of revision without loss of its distinctive value. The King James Version of the Bible is still alive and vital to millions who read it.

The American Standard Version is the English Revised Version edited by a committee of American biblical scholars. The somewhat unusual procedure followed in the preparation of this version is revealed in its descriptive title as published by Thomas Nelson and Sons in 1901: *The Holy Bible containing the Old and New Testaments translated out of the original tongues, being the version set forth* A.D. *1611 compared with the most ancient authorities and revised* A.D. *1881–1885. Newly edited by the American Revision Committee* A.D. *1901, Standard Edition.*

Although the American Standard Version is somewhat more accurate and less literalistic than the English Revised Version published in 1885, the two versions are substantially similar in content.

The American Standard Version is based upon a far more adequate knowledge of the Greek text of the New Testament than was available to the scholars who produced the King James Version.

---

[3] Brooke Foss Westcott, *A General View of the History of the English Bible* (New York: The Macmillan Co., 1927), p. 274.

Furthermore, it clarified a large number of obscure passages in the King James Version, translated Hebrew poetry as poetry, and included exceptionally helpful marginal references. Unfortunately, it failed to retain the literary excellence of the King James Version and provided an awkward word-for-word translation of the Greek text with little regard for the order of words in the English language. For this reason its scholarly value has often been overlooked, and its superficial deficiencies have been magnified. The American Standard Version of the Bible is a product and a producer of sound biblical scholarship.

The Revised Standard Version is an excellent translation of the best text of the Bible available at the middle of the twentieth century. It utilizes the results of thorough biblical scholarship and recovers the dignity and beauty of the King James Version.

This translation of the Bible by American scholars expresses the message of the Bible in the language of this generation. A. T. Robertson frequently told his students that "language is made by the people who use it." More recently Donald F. Ackland has reminded us of the dynamic quality of the English language and has stated that, "unless the Bible is to reflect an outmoded vocabulary, largely unintelligible to today's generation, it must be constantly reviewed and revised." [4] One of the achievements of the Revised Standard Version is the expression of the message of the Bible in clear and contemporary English.

The policies and procedures used in the preparation of the Revised Standard Version are widely known and appreciated. A committee of fifteen scholars appointed by the International Council of Religious Education recommended that a thorough revision of the American Standard Version be made, and in 1937 the council approved a plan for the revision. A committee of thirty-two scholars from the faculties of twenty universities and theological seminaries was invited to participate in the revision with Dean Luther A. Weigle of Yale University as chairman of the committee. Three to five members of the revision committee were to be selected for their competence in English literature, public worship, or religious education. All other members were to be selected on the basis of their competence as biblical scholars. The committee was authorized by the

---

[4] Donald F. Ackland, "One Bible—Many Versions," *The Church Library Magazine*, 1967, p. 2.

council to utilize the "best results of modern scholarship as to the meaning of the Scriptures," to preserve the literary qualities of the King James Version, and to translate the biblical texts into English diction "designed for use in public and private worship."

The translators of the Revised Standard Version made use of the latest discoveries regarding the text and vocabulary of the biblical languages. They decided, for example, to use thirteen readings drawn from the manuscript of Isaiah, which is one of the best preserved manuscripts of the Dead Sea scrolls discovered in 1947. On the basis of evidence available in the Chester Beatty Papyri discovered in 1931, they translated Romans 8:28 as follows: "We know that in everything God works for good with those who love him."

An illustration of the way in which the meaning of words in the English language has changed during the past three hundred and fifty years may be seen in a comparison of the translation of Philippians 1:8 in the King James Version and in the Revised Standard Version:

> For God is my record, how greatly I long after you all in the bowels of Jesus Christ (KJV).

> For God is my witness, how I yearn for you all with the affection of Christ Jesus (RSV).

An example of the quest for an accurate translation in excellent English diction is seen in a comparison of the translation of 1 Corinthians 9:24–27 in the King James and Revised Standard versions:

> Know ye not that they which run in a race run all, but one receiveth the prize? So run, that ye may obtain. And every man that striveth for the mastery is temperate in all things. Now they do it to obtain a corruptible crown; but we an incorruptible. I therefore so run, not as uncertainly; so fight I, not as one that beateth the air: But I keep under my body, and bring it into subjection: lest that by any means, when I have preached to others, I myself should be a castaway.
>
> —KJV

> Do you not know that in a race all the runners compete, but only one receives the prize? So run that you may obtain it. Every athlete exercises self-control in all things. They do it to receive a perishable wreath, but we an imperishable. Well, I do not run aimlessly, I do not box as one beating the air; but I pommel my body and subdue it, lest after preaching to others I myself should be disqualified.
>
> —RSV

What versions are to be used in a serious study of the Bible and why? Equally devout persons answer this question differently. These differences are to be respected. On the basis of the supreme importance of a correct and comprehensive text of the Bible, and of the value of clarity and precision in the use of the English language today, I think it wise to use the Revised Standard Version as the text for study with the American Standard Version and the King James Version open at the same place for instantaneous comparison and with four or five of the relatively recent translations within arm's reach.

You may want to consider purchasing and using in your study translations from the following list:

The New Testament in Modern Speech (Pilgrim Press, 1903; a fourth revised edition, 1924): This version was prepared by R. F. Weymouth, an English Baptist scholar.

The Bible: a New Translation by James Moffatt (Harper and Brothers): This translation was first published in 1922 and was revised in 1939. This is the work of a good scholar, but it is often a paraphrase rather than a close translation. The language is excellent.

The Bible, an American Translation: Primarily the work of Powis Smith (Old Testament) and Edgar J. Goodspeed, this translation first appeared in 1931. Its purpose was to present the Bible in the American idiom.

New American Standard Bible: The ASV New Testament has recently been revised and published by the Lockman Foundation in California. This version more nearly reflects current English usage and takes into account the latest discoveries in biblical archaeology. Scholars are now at work on the Old Testament.

The Centenary Translation of the New Testament was published in 1924 to commemorate the centennial of the American Baptist Bible Society. Translated by Helen Barrett Montgomery, this work is notable for the way it brings out the force of the tenses of Greek verbs.

The New Testament in Modern English: The work of J. B. Phillips, Anglican scholar, this translation is one of the most readable of all English versions. While he did paraphrase at times, his work conveys the true meaning of the Bible passages. His translation of Paul's letters is especially rich. It was published by Macmillan in 1958.

The New English Bible: This work was planned and directed by all the leading denominations in Britain. It was published by Oxford and Cambridge in 1961. This translation is fresh and appealing, though sometimes the American will be confused by the use of British idioms.

The New Testament in the Language of the People: First published in 1937, Charles B. Williams' translation was later released in 1949 by Moody Press. A Southern Baptist did this work which preserves the flavor of the original Greek diction and style in contemporary English.

The Amplified Bible: This is not a new translation, for it uses the King James Version, giving various shades of many key words in the text. When used with good judgment, this version can be helpful. However, the student needs to understand that the art of Bible interpretation depends on more than selecting one of several meanings.

The New Testament in Today's English Version: This book is better known by its popular paperback title *Good News for Modern Man.* It has experienced popularity probably unprecedented in Christian history. Millions of copies have been sold and given away since it was published in 1966 by the American Bible Society. The basic text was translated by Robert G. Bratcher, a Southern Baptist, and the line drawings were prepared by Annie Vallotton, a French artist.

TOOLS FOR BIBLE STUDY

We have books prepared by biblical scholars to assist us in a systematic and thorough study of the Bible in the English language. In addition to their technical work on the text and translation of the Bible, biblical scholars have provided tools for effective Bible study. These can be purchased through the Baptist Book Store in your area; and, although they are imperfect, they can be used constructively by the intelligent and reverent student of the Bible.

In the United States, the cost of books has advanced rapidly in recent years, and these tools for Bible study are expensive. Fortunately, possession of only a few of these tools will make possible a depth study of the message of the Bible in the English language. It is helpful for the Bible student to own a small number of books and to borrow additional ones from the church library or from a public library in the community.

For the kind of Bible study outlined in this book, the student needs a copy of the King James Version and the Revised Standard Version of the Bible. (The American Standard Version would also be helpful.) It is in the Bible itself and not in books about the Bible, important as they are, that we come face to face with the primary documents of the Christian faith.

In almost every type of Bible study a student needs a concordance. If he uses primarily the King James Version or the American Standard Version, a copy of *Cruden's Complete Concordance* is normally adequate. This concordance is not exhaustive, but it includes most of the essential words of the Bible and is available in relatively inexpensive editions. I have used it since 1926 and have never failed to locate the word or passage for which I was searching.

If the student uses the Revised Standard Version as the biblical text in his study, he may wish to consider the purchase of *Nelson's Complete Concordance of the Revised Standard Version Bible* compiled under the supervision of John W. Ellison. The rapid acceptance of the Revised Standard Version, which contains many words not in other editions of the Bible, created the need for a new concordance. The preparation of a complete and accurate concordance by a biblical scholar usually requires approximately twenty-five years. In view of these considerations, it was decided to use electronic assistance. As a result, this concordance is exhaustive but not analytical. The electronic computer enabled a group of editors to produce quickly a complete concordance directly related to the Revised Standard Version. This is a large and somewhat expensive volume; but it is very helpful, not only in the location of passages, but also in the identification of key words in the Revised Standard Version.

An almost indispensable tool to serious Bible study is a Bible dictionary. *Harper's Bible Dictionary,* edited by Madeleine S. Miller and J. Lane Miller in consultation with eminent biblical scholars, including competent archaeologists, is an excellent one-volume dictionary of the Bible published by Harper and Brothers in 1952. Although less conservative than some readers might prefer, it is thorough in scholarship, easy to read, and well illustrated. It contains five hundred illustrations, including four hundred photographs and one hundred line drawings. It clarifies many terms directly related to the understanding of the biblical message. I turned to this dictionary for information on forty-four words the first month I used the book and was not disappointed.

The most comprehensive dictionary of the Bible published recently in English is *The Interpreter's Dictionary of the Bible* in four volumes. This extensive and expensive work contains more than seven thousand five hundred entries, including full-length articles on each book of the Bible. The bibliographies following major articles are most valuable.

The Westminster Dictionary of the Bible (Westminster Press, 1944) is regarded by many Bible students as the most useful and up-to-date volume of its kind. Actually, it is a revision of the *Davis Bible Dictionary* which was a standard work for many years.

The New Bible Dictionary (Eerdmans, 1962) was edited by F. F. Bruce and others. It is a solid, conservative work embodying results of recent biblical scholarship.

A Theological Word Book of the Bible, edited by Alan Richardson and published by the Macmillan Company in 1950, clarifies the theological meanings of a relatively large number of the key words of the Bible. The text of the English Revised Version is used, and the intention is to help the ordinary reader understand the meaning of events recorded in the Bible.

The newest book is not always the best book for Bible study. For example, the eleventh edition of the *Encyclopedia Britannica* contains a wealth of material that can be used in the search for a profound understanding of the Bible. Likewise, the one-volume *Columbia Encyclopedia* contains an astonishing amount of background knowledge for the biblical student.

In order to understand the context of biblical events, the student needs a Bible atlas. The *Oxford Bible Atlas,* edited by Herbert G. May with the assistance of R. W. Hamilton and G. N. S. Hunt, published by the Oxford University Press in 1962, portrays the geographical background of biblical history. The maps are adequate and convenient in size, and the text relates the maps to the biblical data.

The Westminster Historical Atlas to the Bible, Revised Edition (edited by George Ernest Wright and Floyd Vivian Filson with an introductory article by W. F. Albright, published by the Westminster Press in 1956) is a product of careful scholarship and can be recommended to the biblical student with confidence. The maps, photographs, and explanatory chapters provide geographical knowledge of biblical lands and of the people who lived there. The usefulness of this atlas is increased by the Index of Sites.

Biblical commentaries are to be selected, purchased, and used with meticulous care. Their purpose is to help the student of the Bible to understand the meaning of the word, phrase, sentence, paragraph, or longer passage under consideration. The intention is to discover as precisely as possible what the author intended to say.

The Layman's Bible Commentary, a series of twenty-five volumes published by the John Knox Press in 1959, is an admirable guide for a study of the Bible. It was written by biblical scholars who knew how to express religious thought clearly and accurately. The volumes are relatively inexpensive.

In many respects, the most adequate commentary series in English is the *International Critical Commentary* on the Holy Scriptures of the Old and New Testaments. *The Interpreter's Bible,* a twelve-volume commentary designed especially for pastors and teachers, makes available results of more recent developments in biblical scholarship. (The latter does not always represent a conservative viewpoint.)

Eleven volumes of the twelve-volume set, *The Broadman Bible Commentary,* are available now. The revised Volume 1 is scheduled for release on May 1, 1973. The Scripture text is printed in full, with an introduction, outline, exegesis, and exposition of each Bible book. The entire work, based upon solid biblical scholarship, emphasizes the redemptive message of the Scriptures and relates to the issues confronting the people of God today.

(See the annotated bibliography for a fuller listing of Bible study tools. See also the current *Baptist Book Store Catalog.*)

In a guest room at a theological seminary in Washington, I once saw a Bible entitled *Holy Bible with Helps.* It was an appropriate title. We need "helps" in order to understand, to interpret, and to live by the message of the Bible. We need the help available in translations of the Bible, a concordance, a Bible dictionary, a Bible atlas, and carefully selected commentaries. Money spent for these tools to be used in serious study of the Bible is wisely and productively invested.

A pediatrician who examines children with great care and interprets them to their parents, and who directs a study of the Bible by a group of young people in a Sunday School class, decided to secure the essential tools for effective Bible study. He told his wife that he would like for his birthday and Christmas gifts each year to be a concordance of the Bible, a Bible dictionary, a Bible atlas, or a commentary on a book of the Bible. This is one way to secure the essential tools of Bible study without undue pressure upon the family budget. (For a fuller explanation of how to use Bible commentaries, see pp. 142–45.)

QUALIFICATIONS FOR BIBLE STUDY

In addition to an accurate translation of the Bible in up-to-date English and the instruments or tools provided by biblical scholarship, what personal qualifications are required for effective Bible study?

Disciplined Minds

We must have disciplined minds and take the opportunity to listen to what God is saying to us through the Bible. Intelligence is the ability to learn, and memory is the capacity to recall past experience. These capabilities of the mind equip us to focus attention upon biblical truth, to reflect upon the record of what God has said to men in the past, and to discover what he is saying to us today.

At our best moments we bring powerful emotions under the control of intelligence and use our minds in an effort to understand the purpose of God as it is set forth in the Bible. This delivers us from extreme arrogance and pride and prepares us to discern what obedience to God's will is and what it requires.

The productive servant of God studies the Bible with a teachable mind and earnestly desires not only to discover the truth but also to live by it as a disciple of Jesus Christ. The disciplined mind, eager to receive and respond to the message of the Bible, recognizes the sequence of thought, the consistency of religious insight, and the invitation to faithful obedience to God in the pages of the Old and New Testaments.

Creative imagination is a constructive force in the appropriation of the religious insights of the Bible and in the search for a clear understanding of the relation of these insights to the current issues. In the honest effort to hear what God is saying today, the exercise of creative imagination does not displace the fruits of scientific study of biblical documents and of human society, but it illuminates and uses them. Coleridge, who studied the processes involved in the writing of poetry and in literary criticism, defined imagination as the power of human perception, the power of the mind to re-create and shape, and declared that imagination brings "the whole soul of man into activity." The alert and devout mind appropriates religious insights by reflection upon decisive action at crucial moments in the events recorded in the Bible and uses these insights to gain a deeper perception of a current situation, to shape and modify interpersonal relations, to create community in harmony with the mind of Christ.

Christian Fellowship

We are members of the Christian fellowship in which the Bible is studied and interpreted. We read the Bible in the privacy of the home and in the fellowship of the family as a whole, but we also study it in a larger community of faith. The primary unit of the community of believers is the local church, and a study of the Bible in the church increases our knowledge of how it was written, how it was preserved and transmitted to us, and what God is saying to his people through its pages today.

In the Christian community, we study the Bible in the mood of faith and prayer. In the presence of God and of persons who believe in him, we open the Bible and read it with an attitude of expectancy. It stimulates us to think for ourselves, to see ourselves as we are before God and in relation to our neighbors, and to pray for forgiveness and guidance. It teaches us that "we are members one of another" (Eph. 4:25, RSV) and encourages us to speak the truth in love.

Guidance of the Holy Spirit

We are guided and sustained by the Holy Spirit in the study of the Bible. The Bible was written by men under the inspiration of the Holy Spirit. It has been preserved, translated, and interpreted by men under the guidance of the Holy Spirit. We receive its message into our hearts and obey it by the help of the Holy Spirit. "He who was present when the events recorded in the Bible took place and who inspired the writers who recorded them is the very same Holy Spirit who works in our lives today. He takes the message and the events and makes them live with meaning for us in our particular life-situation. Christ promised his disciples that the Holy Spirit would continually teach and reveal the things of God." [5]

---

[5] Howard P. Colson, *Preparing to Teach the Bible* (Nashville: Convention Press, 1959), p. 92.

The concept of the partnership of the Holy Spirit in Bible study is no groundless hope. It is a hope based on the clear promise of our Lord: "I have yet many things to say unto you, but ye cannot bear them now. Howbeit when he, the Spirit of truth, is come, he will guide you into all truth: for he shall not speak of himself; but whatsoever he shall hear, that shall he speak: and he will shew you things to come. He shall glorify me: for he shall receive of mine, and shall shew it unto you" (John 16:12–14).

The writers of the New Testament remind us of three ways by which men have mistreated the Holy Spirit. They have resisted him (Acts 7:51), grieved him (Eph. 4:30), and quenched him (1 Thess. 5:19). This kind of behavior is detrimental to any effective study of the Bible in home and church.

In order to understand, appreciate, and live by the moral and religious insights set forth in the Bible, we are to study it with disciplined minds in the Christian fellowship and under the guidance of the Holy Spirit. This requires intelligence, energy, and faith. It leads to a deeper knowledge of God, stimulates growth in Christian maturity, and keeps open the channel of communication with great religious thinkers.

**Enrichment Resources
for Chapter 2**

Resources for Bible Study

Why Different Versions?—*Robert A. Baker*
Chart of the English Bible

Why Different Versions? [1]

Robert A. Baker

How familiar are you with the various versions of the Bible? Does it perplex you to notice that some of these versions seem to say something different from what you understand the King James Version to mean? Have you wondered how this situation affects the doctrine of the inspiration of the Bible?

If these matters have caused any problem for you, this article may help you to get a firm understanding of the entire question of versions. At the same time, it may help you to become familiar with most of the important English translations of the Bible.

How Versions Help

Bible students have always recognized the value of different translations of the Bible. Early in the Christian era, Origen of Alexandria (born about A.D. 185) gathered a number of different versions of the Scriptures to compare them for serious study. Since his day, there have been many collections of different translations of the Bible to be used as an aid in studying the Bible. For those who use only the English tongue, the various modern versions of the Bible can be very valuable.

Notice some of the reasons for new translations of the Bible into other tongues, including the English.

Archaeological findings.—Doubtless you are familiar with the fact that Bible scholars are constantly excavating in the Bible lands in an effort to unearth the cities and cultures described in the Bible. New information is being found about the customs and the living conditions of the people, for example, who walked the streets of Jerusalem about the time of Jesus and his disciples.

Many of the references in the New Testament, which once were rather vague in their meaning, have now become clear because of the research by archaeologists who have been able to recover the remains of an earlier civilization. With this information, it is possible to make a much better translation of the Bible.

New manuscripts.—Our English Bible is a translation, of

[1] Robert A. Baker, *The Bible—The Book That Lives*, © 1965, The Sunday School Board of the SBC, pp. 69–74. This article was adapted by permission. Dr. Baker is professor of church history, Southwestern Baptist Theological Seminary, Fort Worth, Texas.

course, of copies of manuscripts of books of the Bible gathered from every part of the world. We do not possess the original book of Romans or any other of the original writings; but we have hundreds of copies of the Bible, in whole or in part, gathered from various parts of the world.

Scholars are constantly alert to the possibility of finding additional ancient copies of any part of our Bible, in order that we might compare the reading of the new manuscript with the copies we now possess. The Dead Sea scrolls were a rare find of this type of manuscript. In our own day, these manuscripts, including portions of just about every book of the Old Testament, as well as other writings dating from before the birth of Christ, were found in caves not far from Jerusalem. It should bring a sense of assurance to Christians everywhere to learn that the Old Testament texts discovered there are practically identical with our best Old Testament texts. New versions in English can help reflect findings of the latest discoveries of manuscripts.

Linguistic skill.—Occasionally a person comes along who is gifted of God in linguistic ability. He may spend his entire life studying the Hebrew or Greek language and then be able in his translations to bring out truths that no one else has discovered.

An example is the case of Charles B. Williams, a Baptist scholar who made an excellent translation of the New Testament into English. He was especially gifted in his ability to understand the meaning of Greek verbs. His ability to translate this part of the Greek language into English has provided a very fine help for every Bible student. [*Today's English Version* is a more recent example of a translation in the language of the people.]

Modern language.—Has it occurred to you that language, like anything else in common use, may wear out? This is one of the chief reasons why need arose for a more current version of the Bible than the King James Version. During the several centuries since it was translated, more than two hundred and fifty words have lost their original meaning; and many new words have been added to the English language which can say more clearly what is meant.

Literary style.—Furthermore, occasionally there is a man or woman who is gifted in his ability to use the English language. Such persons have drawn upon this ability of expression to translate into the English tongue the deep truths of the original languages. In so doing, they have produced a clear and beautiful interpretation of the Bible. (Mrs. Helen Montgomery had such ability.)

Study helps.—Any person who has done much Bible study will welcome a new version. The Bible student recognizes that the original revelation was given in Hebrew, Greek and possibly Aramaic. The more different translations he has of a particular verse, the better able he is to see the different emphases and aspects found in the original words of the Bible.

Have you ever wondered why a minister needs to go to a seminary? Not only does his course of study include preaching, church history, theology, and pastoral ministry; but he needs to learn Hebrew and Greek in order that he may interpret the original Scriptures and their meaning. However, even one who has studied Hebrew and Greek welcomes every new version of the Bible, because it suggests to him new and significant insights.

A special class of readers.—Some versions of the Bible have been prepared for use by a particular denominational group. For example, the Roman Catholic Church has its own translation for its members.

Other versions have been prepared from a very limited vocabulary, so that people of limited education may be able to understand it.

The Amplified Bible has also been produced, showing several possibilities of reading for various words. This version was produced to help the readers see the different meanings found in the original words of the Bible.

Which Version Is Right?

As an illustration of the helpfulness of different versions, let us take a familiar passage and illustrate how each version can make its own particular contribution to understanding the passage.

John 1:11–13 reads as follows in the King James Version:

> **He came unto his own, and his own received him not. But as many as received him, to them gave he power to become the sons of God, even to them that believe on his name: which were born, not of blood, nor of the will of the flesh, nor of the will of man, but of God.**

In the American Standard Version of 1901, this verse reads as follows:

He came unto his own, and they that were his own received
him not. But as many as received him, to them gave he the right
to become children of God, even to them that believe on his name:
who were born, not of blood, nor of the will of the flesh, nor
of the will of man, but of God.

In the Revised Standard Version, this verse reads:

He came to his own home, and his own people received him
not. But to all who received him, who believed in his name, he
gave power to become children of God; who were born, not of
blood nor of the will of the flesh nor of the will of man, but of
God.

In *The Bible: An American Translation,* this verse reads:

He came to his home, and his own family did not welcome
him. But to all who did receive him and believe in him he gave
the right to become children of God, owing their birth not to nature nor to any human or physical impulse, but to God.

In *The New English Bible,* this passage reads:

He entered his own realm, and his own would not receive
him. But to all who did receive him, to those who have yielded
him their allegiance, he gave the right to become children of God,
not born of any human stock, or by the fleshly desire of a human
father, but the offspring of God himself.

If you were able to read the Greek text, you would have an
appreciation of each one of these translations into English, because
each one brings out a little different aspect of what the original text
actually says. It is very difficult to say in one English translation
everything that the inspired Greek text contains.

Now which one is right? The answer must be that all of them are
helpful. What does this do, then, to our doctrine of inspiration? The
answer is that God did not promise to inspire those who translate or
copy the Bible.

In Nehemiah 8:1–8, Ezra the scribe read the book of the Law in
the Hebrew tongue to the congregation. Some of the people spoke
Aramaic, so Ezra provided men to translate the Hebrew into Aramaic. The record does not state that God inspired these translators
in order that the Aramaic translation could be called inspired.

We believe it was the original message of God that was inspired.
We should get as close to the original meaning of the best texts of the
Hebrew and Greek as possible.

It should be said, however, that many Bible scholars have been
so impressed by the preservation of the Bible through many centuries,

despite the efforts of the enemies to destroy it and its friends to hide it, that they have a conviction that God's hand has been thrust into history to protect his Word.

Spiritual Results of Varied Versions

Is it of any significance for Christians that we have so many different English versions of the Bible?

Additional versions aid in understanding what the inspired writers were saying.—It is almost impossible to put into a single translation the entire meaning contained in any part of the Bible. Both the original Hebrew and Greek were very colorful languages, suitable for delicate gradations and diverse literary forms. In addition, since the inspired revelation was made for the common people, it tends to introduce colloquialisms and localisms.

Under the circumstances, it is helpful to have a dozen translations of a particular passage as a means of grasping all that it says.

These versions are of great assistance to the Bible student.—The average layman does not read Hebrew and Greek. A careful study of versions, however, can go far to remedy this lack. Meanings are suggested that are often overlooked in the familiar language of the King James Version.

You will not agree with all translations. Sometimes minor variations will vex you; sometimes radical departures will incense you. No matter! Take the help that is given and discard the chaff.

More people will be influenced by the Bible as additional versions are produced.—Some readers like the beauty and dignity of the King James Version; others are thrilled by the clarity of modern translations. Many people read the Bible in one version who would not read it at all in another version. In all, nothing but good can come from continuing to produce the Bible in many versions.

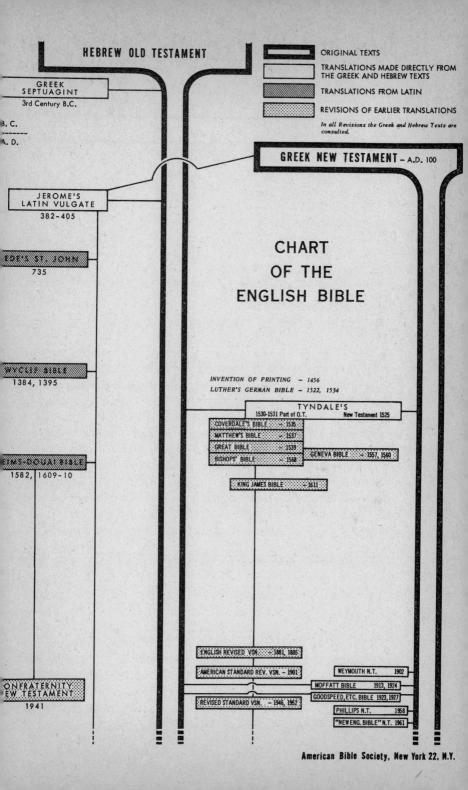

HEBREW OLD TESTAMENT

ORIGINAL TEXTS

TRANSLATIONS MADE DIRECTLY FROM THE GREEK AND HEBREW TEXTS

TRANSLATIONS FROM LATIN

REVISIONS OF EARLIER TRANSLATIONS

In all Revisions the Greek and Hebrew Texts are consulted.

GREEK
SEPTUAGINT
3rd Century B.C.

B. C.
A. D.

GREEK NEW TESTAMENT – A.D. 100

JEROME'S
LATIN VULGATE
382–405

EDE'S ST. JOHN
735

CHART
OF THE
ENGLISH BIBLE

WYCLIF BIBLE
1384, 1395

INVENTION OF PRINTING – 1456
LUTHER'S GERMAN BIBLE – 1522, 1534

TYNDALE'S
1530-1531 Part of O.T.   New Testament 1525

COVERDALE'S BIBLE   1535
MATTHEW'S BIBLE   1537
GREAT BIBLE   1539
BISHOPS' BIBLE   1568   GENEVA BIBLE   – 1557, 1560

EIMS-DOUAI BIBLE
1582, 1609–10

KING JAMES BIBLE   – 1611

ENGLISH REVISED VSN. – 1881, 1885

AMERICAN STANDARD REV. VSN. – 1901   WEYMOUTH N.T.   1902

MOFFATT BIBLE   1913, 1924

GOODSPEED, ETC. BIBLE 1923, 1927

ONFRATERNITY
EW TESTAMENT
1941

REVISED STANDARD VSN. – 1946, 1952

PHILLIPS N.T.   1958

"NEW ENG. BIBLE" N.T. 1961

American Bible Society, New York 22, N.Y.

CHAPTER THREE

Interpretation
of the Bible

It is appropriate to distinguish between reading the Bible, study-ing the Bible, and interpreting the Bible. A person may read the Bible by perusing, silently or aloud, any part of the Old Testament or the New Testament. A serious study of the Bible requires *concentration of the mind upon a specific passage, poring over the words and phrases,* and *using the best available tools of biblical scholarship* in an honest effort to learn as precisely as possible what the writer intended to communicate in the historical situation within which he wrote. An interpretation of a biblical passage is an explanation of its meaning and significance. These three interrelated processes are involved in the quest for an understanding of God's redemptive action and man's response as recorded in the Bible.

The process of interpreting the Bible includes the passage to be interpreted, the interpreter, and the person or persons to whom the interpretation is communicated. The interpreter may be a translator of the Bible, the author of a commentary on a book of the Bible, a biblical theologian, a pastor, a Sunday School teacher, or a parent in a Christian family. Howard P. Colson has delineated the qualifica-tions of the interpreter as: (1) "a regenerate life," (2) "a worthy purpose," (3) "an open mind," (4) "respect for his own competency under God," and (5) "dependence upon the Holy Spirit." [1]

---

[1] Howard P. Colson, *Preparing to Teach the Bible* (Nashville: Convention Press, 1959), pp. 45–48.

The role of the mother as a biblical interpreter merits more attention than it has received. Children are excellent observers but inadequate interpreters. At teachable moments in the process of human growth, they ask religious questions. In response to these questions the mother has an opportunity to listen thoughtfully, to keep the channel of communication open, to present to the mind of her child what she has learned from biblical writers, and to interpret life in the perspective of the mind of Christ.

Although the central theme of the message of the Bible is intelligible to the reverent and thoughtful reader, it is of help to hear interpretations of what the message meant to those to whom it was first addressed and what it means to those who hear it in contemporary culture. Philip asked the eunuch who was reading Isaiah, "Do you understand what you are reading?" and the answer was, "How can I, unless some one guides me?" (Acts 8:30–31, RSV). This question is raised urgently today. How are we to understand the religious message of the Bible in a secular age? How are we to *interpret* the events recorded in the Bible and the types of literature used by biblical writers?

PRINCIPLES OF INTERPRETATION

If you want to understand the Bible, you must read it with a teachable mind, according to a sensible plan, with the eyes of faith, and with the aid of the tools of biblical scholarship. Read it with your family, with friends, and in the fellowship of your church. Read it when you are alone and have time to think seriously about your own life and work and what God is saying to your soul through the message of the biblical writers. In this way you will be brought face to face with what the Bible says and what it means to you.

As you read and ponder the meaning of the Bible for yourself, you will probably come upon a few sections in this collection of sixty-six books which seem to be remote and incomprehensible. At the same time, you will discover or rediscover the throbbing life and power of the message of the Bible. You will encounter the living God whose authentic word brings you to your knees in adoration and confession and to your feet for constructive and creative participation in the needful work of the world. This does not mean that you worship the Bible. It means that you worship the God and Father of the Lord Jesus Christ, who speaks to you through the Bible, who illuminates and empowers your mind, and whose love burns like a flame in your heart.

In your home, in your Sunday School class, and in other groups to which you belong you will be asked from time to time what the Bible says and what the message of the Bible means concerning particular subjects and issues. In these situations you will be an interpreter of the Bible, and it will be helpful for you to be acquainted with the principles of biblical interpretation. A knowledge of the principles of biblical interpretation which have been clarified and used by great biblical scholars and theologians will not enable you to do the technical work of a biblical scholar or theologian. Such knowledge will, however, enable you to think straight and to speak wisely about what the Bible says and means.

Examine Words and Historical Setting

A reliable interpretation of a passage of the Bible begins with an honest and intensive examination of the words the biblical writer used, the historical setting in which he used them, and the message he intended to convey by them. This is an exceptionally difficult task. It requires a knowledge of the biblical languages and of the history of an ancient people. It requires some understanding of the processes involved in a grammatical and historical analysis of a biblical text in the light of its context.

This method of interpreting a biblical passage is based squarely upon what the words of the passage most plainly mean in the perspective of the historical situation in which they were originally spoken or written. The Bible student, with the aid of whatever tools for such an investigation are available to him, determines as honestly and accurately as he can what Amos or Jeremiah or Paul or James intended to say and the situation in which he said it.

Most laymen are not equipped for this kind of scientific analysis of a passage of the Bible. However, all of us have access to the fruits of biblical scholarship and can learn with a reasonable degree of precision the plain meaning of a biblical passage. For example, the translations of the Old Testament in contemporary English are in some respects interpretations of what the text of the Bible means. The translators have examined with personal integrity and technical competence the words used by the biblical writers as they appear in the best available manuscripts. Then they translated these words into the

English language. Furthermore, anyone can use dictionaries and commentaries in which biblical words are examined and explained. We
can all consult historical Bible atlases to locate on a map the sites at
which actions recorded in the Bible took place. Such books can help
us to secure scholarly information concerning the historical situations
related to books of the Bible. Aided by these tools of biblical scholarship, we can read the Bible with understanding and interpret the
meaning of most of its passages.

At least three directives for Bible study are derived from the
historical principle of biblical interpretation.

*Seek diligently to understand what each biblical writer meant by
the words and phrases he used.*—For example, Paul wrote: "So faith,
hope, love abide, these three; but the greatest of these is love" (1
Cor. 13:13, RSV). What did he mean by the word "faith"? He was a
great Christian thinker, writing under the guidance of the Holy Spirit,
and he used a superlative: "the greatest of these is love." What did he
mean by the word "love"? In order to understand and to interpret
adequately Paul's message to the Christians at Corinth, we must determine as accurately as we can what he meant by the words faith, hope,
and love.

Interpret the words of a biblical text in their context.—The
immediate context of a word is the paragraph in which the word is
used. The remote context is the book of the Bible in which the word
is used. In some instances, the remote context is defined as the entire
body of writing by the author who used the word. For example, in
order to discover what Paul meant by the word "faith," the student
may examine every paragraph in all of Paul's letters in the New
Testament in which the word is found.

The detachment of a word or a phrase from its context may
create misunderstanding and tempts the interpreter to use irresponsible procedures. A dramatic example would be to lift a phrase out of a
paragraph in Matthew 5 and have Jesus say, "Hate your enemy." Out
of context this phrase is flatly at variance with the spirit of the
Master, but in its proper context it is a meaningful part of the Sermon
on the Mount:

> You have heard that it was said, "You shall love your neighbor and
> hate your enemy." But I say to you, Love you enemies and pray
> for those who persecute you, so that you may be sons of your
> Father who is in heaven; for he makes his sun rise on the evil and
> on the good, and sends rain on the just and on the unjust. For if

you love those who love you, what reward have you? Do not even
the tax collectors do the same? And if you salute only your breth-
ren, what more are you doing than others? Do not even the
Gentiles do the same? You, therefore, must be perfect, as your
heavenly Father is perfect.

—Matthew 5:43–48, RSV

*Learn as much as possible about the historical situation in which
each book of the Bible was written.*—Get acquainted with its author,
if he is known, with the people to whom the book was first addressed,
and with the difficulties and opportunities with which they had to
deal.

Interpret Theologically

The Bible is essentially a religious book, a book about God's
redemptive action and man's response; and, therefore, it is to be
interpreted theologically as well as historically. The primary principle
in a theological interpretation of the Bible is the centrality of Jesus
Christ as the perfect revelation of God.

There is a genuine continuity between the Old and New Testaments. The basis of this continuity is theological and historical. The
living God who revealed his character and purpose in Jesus Christ is
the God who called Abraham, delivered the Israelites from bondage
in Egypt, established a covenant with his people at Sinai, provided a
land in which they might dwell, and spoke to them through the
prophets, calling them to repentance, sustaining them in days of crisis,
keeping alive hope in their hearts as they faced the future. The
promises made to them are fulfilled in Jesus Christ. There is a
distinctive structure of belief in the Old Testament and a distinctive
structure of Christian faith in the New Testament and a dynamic
interrelation of the two Testaments.

A careful study of the Bible as a whole indicates, as Herbert H.
Farmer reminds us, that there is a discontinuity as well as a continuity
between the Old and New Testaments.[2] The central themes of the Old
Testament are reinterpreted in the New Testament in the perspective
of the mind of Christ. The early Christians did not deny the validity
of the religion of Israel as recorded in the Old Testament but affirmed
its fulfilment in Jesus Christ. The continuity and the discontinuity are
seen in God's decisive action in the life, death, and resurrection of
Jesus and the birth of Christianity as a separate religion.

---

[2] Herbert H. Farmer, "The Bible: Its Significance and Authority," *The Interpreter's Bible* (New York: Abingdon-Cokesbury Press, 1952), I, 28.

The historical events recorded in the Bible as a whole are to be interpreted in the perspective of the sovereignty of God. God's mighty acts in the history of Israel are illuminated by his disclosure of himself in Jesus Christ.

The concept of covenant between God and his people is a vital force in the relation between the Old and New Testaments. Indeed, the title page of the New Testament reads, "The New Covenant Commonly Called the New Testament of Our Lord and Saviour Jesus Christ." Jeremiah had promised a new covenant in which the law would be written on man's heart:

> Behold, the days are coming, says the Lord, when I will make a new covenant with the house of Israel and the house of Judah, not like the covenant which I made with their fathers when I took them by the hand to bring them out of the land of Egypt, my covenant which they broke, though I was their husband, says the Lord. But this is the covenant which I will make with the house of Israel after those days, says the Lord: I will put my law within them, and I will write it upon their hearts; and I will be their God, and they shall be my people. And no longer shall each man teach his neighbor and each his brother, saying, "Know the Lord," for they shall all know me, from the least of them to the greatest, says the Lord; for I will forgive their iniquity, and I will remember their sin no more.
>
> —Jeremiah 31:31–34, RSV

The promise of the old covenant was fulfilled in Jesus Christ.

> This is the covenant that I will make with the house of Israel after those days, says the Lord: I will put my laws into their minds, and write them on their hearts, and I will be their God, and they shall be my people. And they shall not teach every one his fellow or every one his brother, saying, "Know the Lord," for all shall know me, from the least of them to the greatest.
>
> —Hebrews 8:10–11, RSV

> The time is fulfilled, and the kingdom of God is at hand; repent, and believe in the gospel.
>
> —Mark 1:15, RSV

> For I am not ashamed of the gospel: it is the power of God for salvation to every one who has faith, to the Jew first and also to the Greek. For in it the righteousness of God is revealed through faith for faith; as it is written, "He who through faith is righteous shall live."
>
> —Romans 1:16–17, RSV

> Therefore, if any one is in Christ, he is a new creation; the old has passed away, behold, the new has come.
>
> —2 Corinthians 5:17, RSV

Study Literary Forms

The Bible contains different types of literature; and, therefore, we study the literary forms through which its religious message is expressed. The literary forms used by the biblical writers include *historical narratives, laws, poems, songs, prophetic sermons, gospels, parables, letters,* and *apocalyptic writings.*

It was not the primary intention of the biblical writers to produce literature but to record a message about God and his people as they were guided and sustained by the Holy Spirit. Accordingly, we are to read the biblical literature with a clear sense of its *purpose.* In particular, we are to read it in the perspective of God's disclosure of himself in Jesus Christ and of man's affirmative or negative response to that disclosure.

It has been reported that workers in a factory producing surgical instruments failed to see the value of their labor because they did not understand the use to be made of the tools. In an effort to overcome this feeling of meaninglessness in their tasks, they were given a guided tour into an operating room where they saw surgeons using the delicate instruments which they had helped to produce. Immediately the quality of their work was improved. They had personal knowledge of the purpose to be achieved by the products of their toil.[3]

We draw attention here to four examples of the literary forms through which the biblical message is communicated.

Historical narrative.—We begin with an example of historical narrative in which an encounter between Nathan and David is recorded with remarkable objectivity and in which Nathan used a parable to rebuke David:

And the Lord sent Nathan to David. He came to him, and said to him, "There were two men in a certain city, the one rich and the other poor. The rich man had very many flocks and herds; but the poor man had nothing but one little ewe lamb, which he had bought. And he brought it up, and it grew up with him and with his children; it used to eat of his morsel, and drink from his cup, and lie in his bosom, and it was like a daughter to him. Now there came a traveler to the rich man, and he was unwilling to take one of his own flock or herd to prepare for the wayfarer who had come to him, but he took the poor man's lamb, and prepared it for the man who had come to him." Then David's anger was greatly kindled against the man; and he said to Nathan, "As the Lord lives, the man who has done this deserves to die; and he shall restore the

[3] Carter Swaim, *Right and Wrong Ways to Use the Bible* (Philadelphia: The Westminster Press, 1953), p. 169.

**lamb fourfold, because he did this thing, and because he had no
pity." Nathan said to David, "You are the man."**
                                                    —2 Samuel 12:1–7, RSV

In order to place this example of a literary form in its appropriate
context, read 2 Samuel 11:1 to 12:31. Here is straightforward narrative in an ancient book in which real events are recorded with clarity
and with the vividness of a firsthand report. The reader is informed of
David's grievous sin, of what Nathan did and said, and of David's
response.

In this masterpiece of ancient historical narrative, we read that,
in the name of God, Nathan, the prophet, rebuked King David for his
sin and that the king repented. Does this plain statement of facts have
any religious or moral meaning? This question takes us beyond
literary and historical inquiry into the realm of theological interpretation. In the perspective of the religion of Israel and the fulfilment of
its hopes in Jesus of Nazareth, we answer the question affirmatively.
The facts reported do have religious and moral meaning. The prophet
had freedom and courage to rebuke a powerful ruler. The king
repented and was forgiven. Furthermore, the promises of God to
King David were fulfilled in Jesus Christ; and the living God who
spoke to David through the prophet Nathan is speaking to us through
the Bible, through the Holy Spirit. He speaks through the fellowship
of believers, and through the tremendous events of our time. He calls
us to repentance, forgives our sins, and gives us freedom and courage
to speak the truth in love. (See pp. 52–56 for enrichment material on
historical narrative.)

Biblical poetry.—In several books of the Bible the writers use
poetry as a literary form for the expression of profound religious
insights and convictions. The insights are connected with the deepest
questions of the human mind and the most serious moral aspirations
and decisions. The psalmist, for example, expressed the living Word
of God in poetry.

This Hebrew poetry with its recurrence of thought in successive
half lines, its linking of sense to sound and form, is difficult to
translate into English. We are greatly in debt to the biblical scholars
who translated the psalms from the Hebrew manuscripts. These
enable us to listen intelligently and humbly to what the ancient writers
were saying about the goodness of God, the dignity and worth of
man, and the right relation of man to his neighbor.

In a large number of psalms, personal faith is placed in the context of corporate worship. The psalmist is glad to be a member of the worshiping community:

> I was glad when they said to me,
> "Let us go to the house of the Lord!"
> —Psalm 122:1, RSV

A psalmist, who wishes to be a permanent member of God's household, expresses the purpose of his mind in a prayer:

> One thing have I asked of the Lord,
>   that will I seek after;
> that I may dwell in the house of the Lord
>   all the days of my life,
> to behold the beauty of the Lord,
>   and to inquire in his temple.
>   —Psalm 27:4, RSV

This psalmist spoke, not as a lighthearted man who ignored the perils of a dangerous situation, but as a mature man whose faith had been tested in adversity. He spoke as one who reckoned with the realities of human existence, and who desired to take his place in the Temple with those who worship God and seek his will. (See pp. 57–62 for further study of Hebrew poetry.)

Parable.—A careful reading of the teachings of Jesus indicates that he used parables as a literary form for the communication of a religious message on the level of human understanding. His parables, as preserved in the New Testament, give us an excellent opportunity to listen to what he said to people in Palestine a little more than nineteen hundred years ago. The messages of the parables are dramatic, authentic, and memorable. How are they to be interpreted?

One of the constructive contributions of biblical scholarship during recent decades is the clarification of the principles to be followed in the interpretation of the parables of Jesus. Attention to these principles should enable us to avoid the pitfalls of scholars and preachers who for a thousand years read into the details of the parables the opinions of their own minds and frequently obscured the mind of Christ. Scholars still do not agree on one interpretation for each parable, of course, but a better understanding of the principles of interpretation has emerged.

The parable as a literary form uses comparison to convey a message. A typical parable presents one single point of comparison. The first principle of interpretation is to identify the one point of comparison and to derive from it the insight set forth in the parable.

The purpose of the parable is to make people think for themselves as some aspect of truth is presented to their minds. Therefore, the one central thought of the parable should be expressed without extensive elaboration. It is anticipated that the person who hears or reads the parable will think about it for himself and make an appropriate response to the message it conveys. A. M. Hunter says that every parable of Jesus was intended to evoke a response and that the question, "What do you think?" is always explicitly stated or implied.[4]

In the effort to understand the teaching of Jesus in a parable, imagination defined as human perception is appropriate and valuable. A person who reads the parables with disciplined imagination does not project into the message of Jesus what is not there, but discovers what is there and responds to it.

An excellent example of a short parable used by Jesus is the parable of the lost coin:

> Or what woman, having ten silver coins, if she loses one coin, does not light a lamp and sweep the house and seek diligently until she finds it? And when she has found it, she calls together her friends and neighbors, saying, "Rejoice with me, for I have found the coin which I had lost."
>
> —Luke 15:8–9, RSV

This parable is true to life in a particular situation. A woman loses a silver coin, lights a lamp, searches diligently, finds the coin, and invites her friends to share her joy. The focal point is the vivid image of a happy woman who has found a lost coin. What is the context in which this parable appears? It is one of three parables in Luke 15 in which the primary theme is God's love for lost persons. The single point of comparison in this short parable is that God's joy over one sinner who repents is like the joy of the woman who found her lost coin.

The interpretation of the parables of Jesus is a delicate and difficult undertaking. It involves historical, literary, and theological considerations. The old arguments about the meaning of details in the literary structure of parabolic teachings, however, should not deter us from reading the parables. Guided by the principles of interpretation

---

[4] A. M. Hunter, *Interpreting the Parables* (London: SCM Press Ltd., 1960), p. 12.

stated above, we can read the parables in the Gospels with understanding and appreciation. They bring us into contact with the mind
of Christ and permit us to see the relation of his insights to the issues
that emerge in daily living. (For a Bible study based on a parable, see
p. 63.)

Apocalypse.—The word apocalypse, which means "revelation"
or "disclosure," is a technical term employed to designate a type of
literature. The origin of apocalyptic literature is somewhat obscure.
The use of symbolism to conceal ideas as well as to express them has
made the interpretation of apocalyptic writing exceptionally difficult.
Furthermore, the dualism, the determinism, and the attitude of indif-
ference or pleasure toward the sufferings of wicked people encoun-
tered in some apocalypses complicate the interpreter's task. Yet
apocalyptic literary forms can be used to express Christian ideas with
precision and power.

The Revelation to John is the only New Testament book that is
totally apocalyptic. It is apocalyptic literature at its best. It has
illuminating affinities with the book of Daniel in the Old Testament
and with 2 Esdras in the Apocrypha. Some of Jesus' recorded teachings are apocalyptic in nature also.

Except for selected passages frequently read at funeral services,
the book of Revelation is probably the most neglected book in the
New Testament. It should be read with understanding, remembering
that it carries a word from God for all men.

Revelation was written amidst a terrible crisis. At least a
minority of the Christians in the region of Asia Minor had refused to
participate in the worship of the Roman emperor. They were in great
peril, and John himself had been exiled to the island of Patmos.

The author used apocalyptic symbolism to express a message of
faith and fortitude. He encouraged his Christian readers with the
assurance that God controls the energy of the universe, that Christ is
central in the lives of his saints, that Jesus is already victorious in
principle over the hostile forces, that the power of Rome will be
defeated, and that God's purpose in Christ will be fulfilled in a new
heaven and a new earth.

We admit that our knowledge of apocalyptic symbolism is limited. Nevertheless, we discern values in the book of Revelation. Its
message summons men to faith in God, encourages affirmative response to the grace of the Lord Jesus Christ, and provides clues to a

Christian understanding of history which merit the most careful exploration. (For a discussion of Daniel and Revelation as apocalyptic literature, see pp. 71–77.)

Literal versus figurative language.—In a section under the heading "Some Suggestions About Special Problems" from the book *Preparing to Teach the Bible,* Howard P. Colson gives these helpful suggestions:

> Every reasonable effort must be made to determine whether a given statement is to be understood literally or figuratively. Of course, many of the Bible passages in poetry and in prose are figurative. For example:
>
> "The mountains and the hills shall break forth before you into singing, and all the trees of the field shall clap their hands" (Isa. 55:12).
>
> One form of figurative language often found is hyberbole; that is, a deliberate overstatement made for the sake of emphasis. For instance: "It is easier for a camel to go through the eye of a needle, than for a rich man to enter into the kingdom of God" (Mark 10:25). The saying strikingly overstates the truth in order to emphasize the point that there are spiritual perils in the possession of wealth. But that the statement is not to be taken literally is proved by the fact that several rich people became disciples of Jesus (Zacchaeus, for example) and also by his own saying, "With men it is impossible, but not with God" (Mark 10:27).
>
> In the case of figurative passages which have a spiritual meaning, we must be careful not to press the figure too far. For instance, when Jesus said, "Be ye therefore wise as serpents" (Matt. 10:16), he obviously did not mean that we were to try to imitate serpents in every respect. And when he said, "The kingdom of heaven is like unto leaven, which a woman took, and hid in three measures of meal, till the whole was leavened" (Matt. 13:33), we ought not to look for some spiritual truth in the number three or make out that the woman represents the church. In Palestine it would always be a woman and not a man who would be making up bread.[5]

Apparent discrepancies.—Dr. Colson includes another discussion which the Bible student should find most helpful in his search for an understanding of the Scriptures:

> Many so-called discrepancies in the Bible are only such in appearance. Sometimes two apparently contradictory passages are simply different aspects of the same reality. For example, some people have mistakenly supposed that Paul and James are in opposition to each other on the subject of faith: that Paul teaches salvation by faith, but that James teaches salvation by works. But a careful study of both writers will show that James emphasized

---

[5] Colson, op. cit., pp. 59–60.

works not as a means of salvation but as its proof, and that Paul, with all his emphasis on justification by faith alone, also stresses good works as the outgrowth of faith, as can be seen in the "practical section" of every one of his epistles. Paul and James are in essential agreement, but each one looks at the same larger truth from a somewhat different standpoint. Each was writing to meet a different need.

When it comes to verbal differences or apparent discrepancies between various accounts of the same incident, we need not be disturbed. No two persons witnessing a given event tell about it in identical language or with identical detail. The fact that there are differences in the various Gospel accounts of events in the life of our Lord should strengthen rather than weaken our faith in the trustworthiness of the writers. If they all agreed in every detail, they might easily be suspected of collusion. Actually, the variations are like the multiple speakers of a stereophonic record player. They give depth and perspective to the presentation and enable the reality of characters and events to be better understood. In most instances each of the Gospel accounts enriches our total picture of the event.[6]

THE UNITY OF THE BIBLE

Although the biblical writers used many types of literature, the unfolding message they expressed is united by strong ties. Indeed, the religious message of the Bible as a whole is characterized by such a high degree of consistency that able and careful scholars write about "the biblical faith" and "the unity of the Bible."

After forthright recognition of the rich variety of thought and action recorded in the Old and New Testaments, we can now affirm that the unity of the religious and moral message of the Bible is more impressive than its diversity. What is the basis of this unity?

The fundamental *unity* of the Bible can be seen (1) *in the revelation of God through his mighty acts in the history of Israel,* and (2) *in the fulfilment of the promise of the law and the prophets in Jesus Christ, in whom the character and purpose of God are perfectly revealed.* Apart from the New Testament the Old Testament is incomplete. Apart from the Old Testament the New Testament cannot be fully understood. The unifying theme is the theme of redemption. The God of all grace, who spoke through the law and the prophets, came in Jesus Christ to visit and to redeem his people.[7]

---

[6] Op. cit., pp. 62–63.

[7] In a general article entitled "The Study of the Bible" in *The One-Volume Bible* Commentary, edited by J. R. Dummelow (New York: The Macmillan Company, 1954), the author states that "the whole Bible centers in Jesus Christ" (p. 137). The article is helpful to Christian laymen who want to read the Bible with understanding and to relate its teaching to daily living.

In the dynamic message of the Bible we feel the personal authority of God. The writers who recorded what God has done for man's salvation in the history of a people and in Jesus Christ were given divine illumination. We are given *insight* as we study the Bible seriously and honestly and as we accept the invitation of Jesus Christ to learn of him and to follow him.

Enrichment Resources
for Chapter 3

Interpretation of the Bible

Historical Narrative—*D. P. Brooks*
Hebrew Poetry—*A. Stuart Arnold*
The Parables of Jesus—*A. Stuart Arnold*
Apocalyptic Literature—*B. A. Sizemore*
Revelation as Apocalyptic Literature—*Kenneth Wolfe*
Interpreting Prophetic Literature—*Roy Honeycutt*
Studying the Miracles of Jesus—*George Thomason*

EDITOR'S NOTE: The material in this section was prepared by these writers to exemplify and amplify the principles which Dr. Binkley set forth in the preceding chapter. They may be read now for enlightenment and used later as guides to private Bible study.

Historical Narrative
D. P. Brooks

Some of the most dramatic narratives in all literature are found in the Bible. For example, consider the story of Jehu's rebellion against Joram, king of Israel and son of the infamous Ahab and Jezebel, as recorded in 2 Kings 9. This one chapter is so full of action and meaning that one stands amazed that so much is crowded into such short compass. "Then Elisha the prophet called one of the sons of the prophets and said to him, 'Gird up your loins, and take this flask of oil in your hand, and go to Ramoth-gilead. And when you arrive, look there for Jehu the son of Jehoshaphat, son of Nimshi; and go in and bid him rise from among his fellows, and lead him to an inner chamber. Then take the flask of oil, and pour it on his head, and say, "Thus says the Lord, I anoint you king over Israel." Then open the door and flee; do not tarry' " (2 Kings 9:1–3, RSV).

The young man did as he was told: "And the young man poured oil on his head, saying to him, 'Thus says the Lord the God of Israel, I anoint you king. . . . You shall strike down the house of Ahab your master, that I may avenge on Jezebel the blood of my servants the prophets. . . .' Then he opened the door, and fled" (2 Kings 9:6–10, RSV).

Jehu told his companions what the young man had done. "Then in haste every man of them took his garment, and put it under him on the bare steps, and they blew the trumpet, and proclaimed, 'Jehu is king' " (2 Kings 9:13, RSV).

Jehu promptly led his troops to Jezreel, where King Joram was staying. "Now the watchman was standing on the tower in Jezreel, and he spied the company of Jehu as he came, and said, 'I see a company.' And Joram said, 'Take a horseman, and send to meet them, and let him say, "Is it peace?" ' So a man on horseback went to meet him, and said, 'Thus says the king, "Is it peace?" ' And Jehu said, 'What have you to do with peace? Turn round and ride behind me' " (2 Kings 9:17–18, RSV). When a second rider from Joram had the same experience, the watchman reported: " 'The driving is

Mr. Brooks is editor of Uniform lesson materials, Adult Section, Sunday School Department, Sunday School Board. Nashville, Tennessee.

like the driving of Jehu the son of Nimshi; for he drives furiously' "
(2 Kings 9:20, RSV).

Now notice the fine touch of the writer: "Joram king of Israel
and Ahaziah king of Judah set out, each in his chariot, and went to
meet Jehu, and met him at the property of Naboth the Jezreelite. And
when Joram saw Jehu, he said, 'Is it peace, Jehu?' He answered,
'What peace can there be, so long as the harlotries and the sorceries
of your mother Jezebel are so many?' Then Joram reined about and
fled, saying to Ahaziah, 'Treachery, O Ahaziah!' And Jehu drew his
bow with his full strength, and shot Joram between the shoulders, so
that the arrow pierced his heart, and he sank in his chariot. Jehu said
to Bidkar his aide, 'Take him up, and cast him on the plot of ground
belonging to Naboth the Jezreelite' " (2 Kings 9:21–25, RSV).

The chapter records Jehu's killing of Ahaziah king of Judah and
closes with the gripping account of the death of Jezebel. All of this in
one chapter!

The writer of Kings did not include this story simply because of
its literary power or its dramatic force. Rather, he was showing how
God moved to turn his people from heathen Baalism. Jehu was the
agent of the Lord in purging the nation of the cancer of Baal worship.
Radical surgery was required.

For the sequel to the story of the overthrow of Baalism in the
Northern Kingdom, turn to 2 Kings 11. Here is the dramatic story of
Athaliah, the daughter of the infamous Jezebel. Athaliah seized
power upon the death of her son Ahaziah and set out to kill all of the
royal family so as to secure her power. Jehosheba snatched young
Joash away and hid him until he was seven years old. In a beautifully
executed plot, Jehoiada the priest led a *coup d'etat* which overthrew
the wicked queen, restored the throne to a descendant of David, and
tried to root out the Baalism Athaliah had imposed on the people.

By these dramatic narratives, the biblical writer revealed God's
action during a time when all seemed lost. With Jezebel in Samaria
and Athaliah in Jerusalem, the situation seemed hopeless. But God is
not a remote sovereign who allows history to run its own course. He
acts through dedicated men to turn history around—to defeat his
enemies and to move on with his plan of redemption.

It seems surprising to Bible students to learn that when the
Hebrews referred to that part of the Old Testament called "the
former prophets," they were referring to Joshua, Judges, 1 and 2

Samuel, and 1 and 2 Kings. Why refer to this historical material as prophecy? The Hebrews rightly saw that this was not just fragments of historical material, such as one would find in any nation. Rather, this is interpreted history, history seen as the action of God and the responses of men. Here is salvation history, in which God reveals his power, his purpose, and himself.

The New Testament has a large section of historical narratives, too. The four Gospels record the actions of Jesus Christ, a real man in an actual human setting. But it is in the book of Acts that we find the largest single block of historical narrative. Luke traced the spread of the Christian religion by reporting solid historical facts that are reliable both as inspired record and as history.

For example, we look at Acts 10, which records one of the pivotal events in the spread of Christianity. "At Caesarea there was a man named Cornelius, a centurion of what was known as the Italian Cohort, a devout man who feared God with all his household, gave alms liberally to the people, and prayed constantly to God. About the ninth hour of the day he saw clearly in a vision an angel of God coming in and saying to him, 'Cornelius.' And he stared at him in terror, and said, 'What is it, Lord?' And he said to him, 'Your prayers and your alms have ascended as a memorial before God. And now send men to Joppa, and bring one Simon who is called Peter'" (10:1–5, RSV).

Cornelius obeyed, and the story picks up the action of Peter: "Peter went up on the housetop to pray, about the sixth hour. And he became hungry and desired something to eat; but while they were preparing it, he fell into a trance and saw the heaven opened, and something descending, like a great sheet, let down by four corners upon the earth. In it were all kinds of animals and reptiles and birds of the air. And there came a voice to him, 'Rise, Peter; kill and eat.' But Peter said, 'No, Lord; for I have never eaten anything that is common or unclean.' And the voice came to him again a second time, 'What God has cleansed, you must not call common.' This happened three times, and the thing was taken up at once to heaven" (10:9–16, RSV).

"Now while Peter was inwardly perplexed as to what the vision which he had seen might mean, behold, the men that were sent by Cornelius . . . stood before the gate. . . . And while Peter was pondering the vision, the Spirit said to him, 'Behold, three men are looking for you. Rise and go down, and accompany them without hesitation; for I have sent them' " (10:17–20, RSV).

The story continues: "When Peter entered, Cornelius met him and fell down at his feet and worshiped him. But Peter lifted him up, saying, 'Stand up; I too am a man.' And as he talked with him, he went in and found many persons gathered; and he said to them, 'You yourselves know how unlawful it is for a Jew to associate with or to visit any one of another nation, but God has shown me that I should not call any man common or unclean' " (10:25–28, RSV). When he had heard Cornelius' story, "Peter opened his mouth and said: 'Truly I perceive that God shows no partiality, but in every nation any one who fears him and does what is right is acceptable to him' " (10:34–35, RSV). After Peter had preached to the Gentile group, "the Holy Spirit fell on all who heard the word. And the believers from among the circumcised who came with Peter were amazed, because the gift of the Holy Spirit had been poured out even on the Gentiles. For they heard them speaking in tongues and extolling God. Then Peter declared, 'Can any one forbid water for baptizing these people who have received the Holy Spirit just as we have?' And he commanded them to be baptized in the name of Jesus Christ" (10:44–48, RSV).

When Dr. Luke chose to incorporate this narrative section in his account of the things Jesus continued to do, he meant for it to carry theological truth. In Acts 1:8 he quoted Jesus as saying: " 'You shall be my witnesses in Jerusalem and in all Judea and Samaria and to the end of the earth' " (RSV). Step by step, the gospel spread out beyond Jerusalem. But the feeling persisted that the gospel was for Jews only. In this special intervention of God in the experience of Peter, we see a break in the restraining and restricting dikes. Violating the traditions of the Jews, Peter was almost dragged by the Spirit to a Gentile group. Against his strong feelings, he declared the gospel to them and saw the miracle of the Holy Spirit coming to transform them. When the showdown came over preaching the gospel to the Gentiles, as recorded in Acts 15, the testimony of Peter in recounting this event helped turn the tide. Christianity could not be contained— it must break all bounds, lower all barriers, include all nations.

Indeed, one who reads Acts as simply the actions of the apostles misses the meaning. Luke was telling about how the Holy Spirit did his work and broke down barriers. True, men and women of faith had

significant roles to play. Simon Peter had to give his consent to the
Spirit's prompting to go to Cornelius. But it was the Holy Spirit who
initiated the series of events that brought the movement toward an
unfettered gospel. *In reading this and all other historical sections of
the New Testament, we need to look beyond the story and see the
revelation of God that is being communicated to those who are open
to his word.*

Hebrew Poetry
A Study in the Psalms
A. Stuart Arnold

The approach to this study will be along two lines. *In the first place, the form of Hebrew poetry is considered. In the second part, the meaning of one psalm is discussed.* Psalm 116 is chosen for this study because it is typical of the characteristics described in the foregoing chapter, and it provides a good example of a personal testimony which found a permanent place in the treasury of public devotion.

The Form of Hebrew Poetry

The modern English reader is familiar with poetry which has rhyme and rhythm. The blank verse of Shakespeare or Milton will also be recognized as poetry because the lines have a regular number of beats. Hebrew poetry has neither rhyme nor rhythm. Its distinctive form is the use of parallels in strophes (verses). Each strophe is made up of two lines, each of the lines carrying closely-linked thoughts. This form stands out clearly in the psalms of praise.

> **Praise the Lord, all nations!**
> **Extol him, all peoples!**
> **—Psalm 117:1** [1]

The poet's skill is seen not only in his right choice of words or in his imagery, but also in his use of the interplay of thought between the parallels of each strophe. He can speed up or slow down the movement of the psalm, define more fully the thought being expressed, or draw the worshiper more deeply into this experience. The skill with which he does this reveals what quality of poet has written the song.

There are many ways in which an interplay can be developed between parallel lines. The second parallel may be used *to repeat* what the first line says. Psalm 91:1 offers a familiar example in its opening verse:

> **He who dwells in the shelter of the Most High,**
> **who abides in the shadow of the Almighty.**

---

[1] All quotations are from the Revised Standard Version, which more clearly shows the poetic form.

Mr. Arnold is a consultant, Extension Activities section, Sunday School Department, the Sunday School Board, Nashville, Tennessee.

No new idea is introduced, but the original thought is repeated in similar terms with only the slightest change in emphasis.

It is difficult, however, to repeat an idea without introducing something new and, consequently, the parallel form may be used *to add* to the original thought some new one which will bring richer understanding. In Psalm 51, the poet is pleading for forgiveness from God. Four verses in the heart of the psalm (vv. 9–12) demonstrate how this repetition with slight additions carries the thought forward so that the first request, "Hide thy face from my sins," is transformed to, "Uphold me with a willing spirit." Without effort the reader is led from a negative to a positive position.

In many instances, this movement of thought is much more rapid, for the poet will use the second parallel clearly *to complete the thought of the first.* An example of this is found in Psalm 102:18:

> **Let this be recorded for a generation to come,**
> **so that a people yet unborn may praise the Lord.**

The thought is continuous and yet the second line fulfils and completes the first, while at the same time it repeats much of its content.

Yet another form of the parallel strophe is found in the type where the second parallel underscores the first *by comparison and contrast.* The final verse of Psalm 1 is a good example:

> **For the Lord knows the way of the righteous,**
> **but the way of the wicked will perish.**

This is a dramatic usage which effectively underlines the assertion being made.

It may be helpful to see how these four forms of parallel appear in the psalm which is to be studied later in this chapter, Psalm 116. The versification of the psalm does somewhat hide the simple parallels, for instance in verses 13–14. All four types are well represented; however, the repeat form is found in verse 3:

> **The snares of death encompassed me;**
> **the pangs of Sheol laid hold on me.**

The thought is not advanced at all in the repetition, but it is in verse 2:

> **Because he inclined his ear to me,**
> **therefore I will call on him as long as I live.**

There the experience of answered prayer leads to the resolve to continue to depend upon it.

The response of the second parallel to the first in verse 4 is a good example of the third type, where the thought is completed.

> **Then I called on the name of the Lord:**
> **"O Lord, I beseech thee, save my life!"**

The use of the parallels in each strophe to compare and contrast is used in the twin verses 10 and 11:

> **I kept my faith, even when I said,**
> **"I am greatly afflicted";**
> **I said in my consternation,**
> **"Men are all a vain hope."**

The Use of Hebrew Poetry

The psalms have sometimes been called "Jesus' hymnbook." Psalms and hymns are written in poetic form for the same reasons. Poetry lends itself to the more adequate expression of the spirit, its longings and its rare moments of fulfilment. It can suggest, by its associations of thought and feeling, more than prosaic words can define. Therefore, in the study of the psalm the reader should seek to respond to the poetry and try to see how the writer, using rich imagery, carefully chosen words, and the interplay of parallel thoughts, can carry him to depths of spiritual experience which confirm or surpass his own.

The poetic form also enabled the congregation to share in a united act of worship. These words were repeated antiphonally in the setting of worship. The first part of the verse would be spoken by the person leading worship and the second by the whole congregation. The parallel prompted the congregation with its words, just as rhythm and rhyme in modern hymns help the congregation to remember words. Music keeps the singing congregation together today; in Hebrew worship, the rhythm was provided in the statement and response of the parallels.

In a group study of the psalms, it is well worthwhile to begin with an antiphonal reading of the psalm. Let the group leader read the first part of the strophe and then let the group answer by reading the second. (A family Bible study might be conducted in this way.) Some slight preparation may have to be made where the verses are not simple parallels. The reading aloud will make the psalm come alive, just as the singing of hymns makes them meaningful, both in public and private devotion.

Psalm 116

Psalm 116 can be divided into four sections:

1. Deliverance from death, verses 1–4
2. Testimony of praise, verses 5–7
3. Deliverance from doubt, verses 8–11
4. Praise in the Temple, verses 12–19

Deliverance from Death

The psalm begins with a word of personal testimony to the faithfulness of God. Because the Lord has responded to the cry of the psalmist, he vows to love him as long as he lives. This may appear to be very selfish and an inadequate reason for making a vow of devotion to the Lord. Yet the poetry of the writer makes the reader understand so much more about his love of God. He is so rich and merciful a God that the cry of an insignificant man was not overlooked by him. The stress at this point is not on what the Lord did to relieve the distress; it is on the fact that he heard (see v. 1).

In verses 3–4, the psalmist tells what his distress was. He had been smitten by some disease, and the hand of death was already upon him. How effective here is the repetition of the anguish in the parallel statements! Just as the animal caught in the snare hastens his death as he struggles, so did the psalmist. Death gnawed within him like pangs of hunger which the dust of Sheol could not satisfy. He was already in the power of death. There is no need for the suggestion, sometimes made, that the condition described was a condition of the spirit rather than of the body. Sickness of the spirit was also present (vv. 8–11), but it was caused by the weakness of the body and the physical suffering endured. Out of this physical weakness the psalmist cries to God, "O Lord, I beseech thee, save my life!"

Testimony of Praise

Without a pause to say how he was delivered, the poet breaks into praise for the goodness of the Lord. The praise, at this stage in the psalm, is intensely personal. He is thrilled by the wonder of the deed done for him. He remembers his insignificance and low condition and glories in the way the Lord cared for him. "Such a God," he reasons, "must be gracious and merciful if he could stoop to save such a one as me!" This is the solid ground for continuing trust. The soul of man can be at peace when he knows that the Lord who cares for him is mighty and merciful.

Gratitude that is rich and spontaneous is a source of strength to the believer. This man was in a very pitiful condition when he asked for help. When he was restored, he did not forget his cry of distress; but, without argument or reasoning, he breaks forth into a song of praise. In that act of praise, he finds the ground for yet greater assurance, "Return, O my soul, to your rest; for the Lord has dealt bountifully with you" (v. 7).

Deliverance from Doubt

This feeling of peace and assurance reminds the psalmist that it was not always so with him. He, therefore, remembers in his song the doubts and fears that came as a result of his physical weakness. Here he breaks away from a double parallel to use a three-line parallel. In the first he states that his physical suffering led to spiritual problems, and then in the next two lines he illustrates what happened. He was full of self-pity and doubt. The sufferings of the flesh challenged his belief in the goodness of God (v. 10). Like Job, he had heard comforters who failed to help, and doubt came.

The psalmist was honest about his self-appraisal and is, therefore, of help to those who read his words. His victory did not come easily. His sufferings brought him those feelings which sufferings usually bring, and he did not pretend that in the midst of his pain he was free from fear and doubt. Sorrow can drive a man to God if he is willing to put his doubts to the test of trust. When a man's anguish is translated into prayer, he has drawn closer to God in an experience which will not easily be shaken by vicissitudes that come later.

Praise in the Temple

The fresh realization of the great work accomplished by the Lord drives the psalmist to a renewal of praise. Here, though, he looks around him to those who share his worship in the Temple. "How can I repay the Lord?" he asks. "I will repay him by a fuller devotion."

Gratitude to God is the basic dynamic of the believer's life. When the present-day Christian has little desire to minister, it is often because he has no deep sense of indebtedness to the Lord. Praise may be given to the doctor who restores a patient; psychological terms may be used to explain how a spiritual malady is overcome; long-practiced habits of physical discipline can be given credit for recovery —anything rather than an open acknowledgment of the activity of the hand of the Lord. Because the psalmist was so conscious of the Lord's goodness to him, he expressed his thanks in public, calling upon all who heard to take notice of his gratitude and of his vow to serve.

How wise, too, is the psalmist's understanding that what the Lord requires in return for his mercy is not a multiplicity of good acts, the giving of alms, the observance of feasts, or obedience to a code of morals. He saw a more fundamental offering in the offering of his love. The other things will follow as a consequence. What the Lord requires first is not a vow to perform external deeds, but a repentance which will result in a transformation without.

Finally, it should be noticed that the psalmist's deep longing was that he should share these wonders of God's grace with as many people as possible. There is a vital place in Christian experience for the intimate personal experience to find expression in public. The psalmist shows that when a man has had a vital contact with God he should share it. Others will be inspired to worship with him and give God the praise; others will be helped to endure in their day of distress and live to praise him.

Notice how the repetitions in parallel of the gratitude and praise of the psalmist draw the whole congregation into his experience. As the modern reader is carried along by his poetry, he also enters into the poet's experience and finds himself joining his voice with that congregation gathered in the Temple on Zion's hill in the climax of the psalm's last verse, "Praise the Lord!"

The Parables of Jesus
Including a Study of Matthew 25
A. Stuart Arnold

"With many such parables he spoke; . . . he did not speak to them without a parable" (Mark 4:33–34, RSV). The parables of Jesus have helped people all through the centuries to understand deep spiritual truths. They contain fundamental truths in pictures that have been readily understood by people of different cultures and ages. Life in the Palestine of Jesus' day was utterly different from life in the contemporary scientific scene. Yet, a study of the parables brings men to an understanding of spiritual truth. One reason for their enduring quality is found in the form of the teaching that Jesus took and used with most supreme skill.

The form of the parable depends upon its immediate link with the ordinary things of life. The story has to tell of what could happen to anybody in the course of his experience. In every generation people have lost things and searched for them until finally they have rejoicingly found them. Therefore, the story of the woman who lost a coin and single-mindedly searched for it in her primitive house is readily understood by the woman who misplaces something in her fashionable executive apartment.

Jesus told many such stories and in each of them preserved an authentic piece of life which has an immediate parallel in every man's experience. He kept them simple and to the point, sketching the background with an economy of line which at once makes the background fade away to let his message stand out with clarity. The road to Jericho, the form of the attack, the preoccupations which dulled the compassion of the passersby—all of the necessary elements in the story of the Samaritan are cleared away in a few phrases. Then the Master lets us look at the central figures as they cross the barriers of race. What would ultimately happen to the prodigal is known by the reader as soon as the story begins; and at every stage the reader can say, no matter when or where he reads, "That is just what would happen!" And then the message strikes home.

This form of teaching is essentially different from that of the allegory. Preachers and expositors through the centuries have been

63

misled in treating the parables as though they were allegorical stories. The allegory is a valid story form of teaching, and it has been used with consummate skill to teach spiritual truths. Perhaps the finest allegory ever written is John Bunyan's *Pilgrim's Progress*. This form of writing is linked to life, but it will readily use an incident that could never happen in life. For instance, the burden of man's sin is represented by the burden on Pilgrim's back. When Pilgrim looks at the cross, the burden falls away and rolls down the hill into the mouth of the empty tomb. The event did not and could not happen in ordinary experience, and yet the reader learns from this imaginary happening that the cross of Jesus sets a man free from the burden of sin. Most allegorical descriptions of the meaning of life (and of events at the end of the age) do not claim the attention of the present-day reader.

It is important to stress the difference between the allegory and the parable. When Bible students treat the parables as though they are allegories, they identify each element of the story and give it a weight it cannot bear. They have sometimes sincerely applied their preconceived notions to the story and have made each part mean something quite precise. The result has not only been complicated but it has also been far from the truth taught in the original setting. Some students have worked out a system of types, making each object stand for the same thing in different stories. This forces the message of the parable into molds never meant for it. In an allegory the writer makes up his imaginative story, bringing in objects and events which would not normally fall together and making things happen outside normal expectation. The understanding depends upon the reader's identification of what the objects and actions stand for in that particular story. In the parable the main characters and events also run parallel to the thing represented, but the details have no peculiar significance. Thus, to say that the prodigal son represents the sinner wandering from God, while the father represents the God who is ready to receive the returning sinner, is clearly legitimate. To force every detail, such as the husks, or the ring, or the robe to mean something is to make the passage say what it does not say.

From this we come to an important truth about the parable as a teaching aid. *The parable is designed to carry one main message and not many*. The question to ask is not, How many wonderful coincidences can I find in this parable? but, *What great theme does this story illustrate?*

Most of the parables grew out of the needs of a specific situation. A lawyer asks, "Who is my neighbor?"; and the story of the good Samaritan follows. When a Pharisee rebelled against a sinful woman's extravagance, Jesus told the story of the two debtors (Luke 7:36–50). On one occasion Jesus was invited to dinner in a Pharisee's house, and Luke said: "Now he told a parable to those who were invited, when he marked how they chose the places of honor" (Luke 14:7, RSV). Then follows the story of the marriage feast. Each story was designed to teach something in a given situation, enabling men to see the consequences of their actions in the situation in which they found themselves. Thus, the stories are kept close to life and have the ring of truth about them.

Yet as each of these stories is told, Jesus lifts the story out of the immediate context to set it in the context of enduring spiritual truth. The use of the local illustration to highlight a deep spiritual truth was such a dominant part of Jesus' teaching that Peter was driven to put this very point into words when he said, " 'Lord, are you telling this parable for us or for all?' " (Luke 12:41, RSV). Jesus did not commit the fallacy of arguing from the particular to the general, but he regularly took the particular incident to illustrate the general truth. The story does not die with the passing of the occasion that prompted it. The occasion which prompted it lives on in the eternal truth it illustrates. Jesus was never guilty of overworking his illustrations (as many modern preachers do when they find a good one!). He took the recognizably true incident and let it say one thing of deep significance. The modern reader of the parable needs to ask what this one thing is, for it will have a real significance for him, too.

To demonstrate what these principles mean for Bible study in the parables of Jesus, an example will be taken from the series found in Matthew 25. In this chapter there are three stories: the virgins and the marriage feast, the talents, and the sheep and the goats. This chapter is chosen for this study because each story presents the student with a different challenge. Yet each of the stories deals with the main theme, namely, the apocalyptic theme of the events at the end of the age.

Only two of these stories are parables. The story of the sheep and the goats is often loosely described as a parable but it is not. It is a prophetic picture of the judgment. Metaphors are used in the picture. "Before him will be gathered all the nations, and he will

separate them one from another as a shepherd separates the sheep
from the goats" (Matt. 25:32, RSV). The use of the metaphors
helped the hearer to fix in mind that in the judgment men will be
divided into one of only two classes, the saved and the condemned.
There are no sheep-goat crossbreeds! After this illustrative clarification is made in the opening of the story, the reference to sheep and
goats is dropped. From this point on Jesus pictured events that would
take place, but he did not illustrate them with a story taken from
ordinary life.

The stories of the virgins and of the talents are parables, for in
them Jesus took normal situations from life and used them to illustrate a spiritual truth. The spiritual truth concerns the problems of the
waiting period before the second coming of Christ.

The parable of the virgins fulfils all the requirements of the
parabolic form. This is an entirely credible story, true to life in each
detail. It reflects customs and conditions of the times, but it does not
make them essential parts of the story. As the story is read, the
happiness and joyful anticipations of any wedding day are conjured
up by the storyteller. The essential message stands out clearly. The
Christian must be prepared for the Lord's return. Some appear to be
ready, but they need to examine themselves to see whether their
spiritual alertness is reality or pretense. This message is timeless and
is carried straight to the mind and will by the clarity of the illustration. The simple, profound truth must not be fogged by trying to see
hidden meanings in such things as the numbers involved, the oil, the
sleep or the vessels, and the lamps. This parable says to the Christian:
Search your heart. Is your inner spiritual experience a reality? Are
you really prepared to meet the Lord?

The parable of the talents (vv. 14-30) presents the student with
an additional fascinating exercise. In Luke 19:12-28 there is the
parable of the pounds. Scholars have long debated whether these two
stories are differing accounts of one story into which divergencies
entered as the story was repeated and the oral tradition built. In
Luke's account, ten servants are given pounds and each of the
servants selected for detailed description is given one pound.
The profit gained by the two faithful ones varied, and the rewards
were varied to fit the profit gained. Matthew has three servants who
receive different sums each, five, two, and one talent. Each of the
faithful ones doubled their holding and received the same reward.

The unfaithful one received the same treatment as in Luke's story, the loss of the privilege of service.

Are these different stories or are they varying accounts of the same story? With many other scholars a Victorian writer, A. B. Bruce, believed that they were not the same; and he saw great significance in the differences. In Luke's story there is the example of degrees of faithful service with equal opportunity. Whereas, in Matthew's account, there is the example of equal service (in doubling the capital) with unequal opportunity. There is undoubtedly spiritual truth here. The comparison of the two accounts challenges the student to consider whether he is making the fullest use of his opportunities in his service to the Lord.

Yet both parables have a common significance. The specific occasion for the telling of the story, according to Matthew's account, was the confusion in the disciples' minds regarding expectations of the coming kingdom. Paul's letter to the Thessalonians shows how eager expectation of the second coming of the Lord led some people to give up all the normal pursuits of life, so that they might be spiritually prepared. Paul enunciated the principle, "Those who do not work do not eat" (2 Thess. 3:10–11). In the parable of the virgins Jesus stressed the need for adequate preparation; and then, with wonderful foresight, went on to remind the disciples that they must fill the waiting time with purposeful, profitable activity.

The really significant message of the parable is not found in the details. It is found in the main theme of labor and reward. Inaction is not the mark of the Christian. He is required to be up and doing, no matter how much or how little he has, no matter what opportunities come his way. If he fills the time with dedicated service, he has his reward—further service, as both Gospels agree. In this further service, the disciple finds his continuing joy. Both parables speak with great force about the warning given to the unprofitable servant. The sentence of condemnation, solemn and serious as it is, was passed because he did not use his stewardship at all, not even by investing the talent in the bank. The question that Jesus was asking is not about gain and loss; it is about faithfulness and unfaithfulness. The question the story poses is, Have you done what you could?

The details of the story convincingly prove the penetrating insights which Jesus had into the thoughts and actions of men. They hold the interest, support the credibility of the story, and urge the reader to go on to the end of the story and then apply its message to himself. There is the perception of the householder who gives the one talent to the fearful man who was afraid to risk even that one. There is the open approach of the faithful ones as they give their account, compared with the devious approach of the third servant (v. 21). The response of the Master, who turns the excuse into deeper condemnation, is so vivid. There is the rich understanding that the best reward, that which produces the greatest joy, for the believer is more service. All these insights bring the believer nearer to the Saviour. They help him to catch the purpose of the story and carry him forward to that place where he will desire to hear the Master's "Well done!" for himself. Therefore, do not be idle but employ your time gloriously for his sake, till he comes!

Apocalyptic Literature
B. A. Sizemore

Apocalyptic literature emerged as a distinct literary type toward the end of the Old Testament period and was produced in Hebrew and Christian communities until about A.D. 100. The most important biblical representatives of this type of literature are the books of Daniel in the Old Testament and Revelation in the New Testament. The word apocalyptic is Greek in origin; and it means "to uncover," or "to reveal." The literature was produced by the people of God against a background of tension and oppression. It often appeared at a time when a disinterested observer might have been inclined to believe that adherents to the faith, Hebrew or Christian, were facing obliteration by powers not only superior to them but devoted to their destruction.

At moments when it appeared that all the external evidence pointed to the failure and disintegration of God's chosen people, the apocalyptists believed that they were permitted to look at the true reality behind the scene. Surface impressions were stripped away, and it was revealed that the terrifying world powers—Greek, Roman, or whatever—stood under the judgment of God. The destiny of God's own people was secure in the purpose of God; purposes now revealed, at least in part, to the apocalyptist.

Though the apocalyptists insisted upon responsible and courageous behavior on the part of the faithful, their principal concern was not so much to warn the people of God's punishment for disobedience, but to reassure them that God was effectively in control of history and that in his ultimate triumph he would vindicate the faithful.

LITERARY CHARACTERISTICS

Because they were directed to a beleaguered minority, and because they gave voice to mysterious other-worldly realities, the apocalyptic writings shared a secretiveness and extrahistorical quality not apparent in most other literary types. Though not always, the message of the apocalyptist was often presented in the form of

Dr. Sizemore is professor of Old Testament Interpretation and Hebrew, Midwestern Baptist Theological Seminary, Kansas City, Missouri.

visions, a literary device which provided a garment in which to clothe
the apocalyptist's dramatic statements about the inner meaning of
history.

Apocalyptic writings abound in symbolism, most notably the
likening of various animals to historical realities. The extensive use of
symbolism, indeed, the whole aura of mystery surrounding apocalyptic literature has opened the gates to a flood of interpretations
throughout the years of Christian history, with many interpreters in
each generation finding instances in which the symbolism speaks of
their own age. This is quite meaningful when the symbols are seen to
speak of continuing realities. It is less so when the symbols are
identified exclusively with the events of a given age with resulting
attempts to predict specifically the unraveling course of human
events.

THEOLOGICAL EMPHASIS

The theological concept which colors every expression of apocalyptic literature is that of the consuming struggle between good and
evil. The writer seems to see heaven and earth and all their inhabi-
tants embroiled in a conflict between the forces of righteousness and
the forces of evil. In biblical apocalypses, God always remains firmly
in control. Yet the forces of evil are nonetheless monstrous and are
capable of bringing great calamity upon the people of God.

The apocalyptists understood the history of their day to be
dominated by the forces of evil; therefore, great suffering was to be
the lot of those who were joined to the forces of God. Times of
trouble, great woes, and tribulation were to be expected as the
conclusion of history drew near. The intervention of God, however,
was viewed as a certainty. The time of dominion by evil, with its
conflict and turmoil, was certain to give way to a new history in which
God firmly established his saints. There was little that the saints could
do to bring in the new age, but they could be courageously faithful as
they awaited God's intervention and deliverance.

Those who wrote apocalyptic literature were pessimistic about
the history in which they were forced to live, but they were quite
optimistic about God's ultimate purposes. They were equally certain
that forces of evil would have no capacity for resistance at the time
God should choose to transform the existing order and bring it into
line with his purposes.

RELEVANCE OF APOCALYPTIC LITERATURE

Apocalyptic literature seems especially to come alive in those situations in which faithful men are able to identify with the hardships of those who first produced this literature. This is true even when the reader is not especially aware of the historical situation in which the apocalypse was born. Oppressed by a world which is insensitive to the activity of God and to the beauty of the Christian gospel, the believer instinctively identifies with the message of those whose experience has penetrated the depth of rejection and loneliness.

Interpreters of apocalyptic literature sometimes feel constrained to go beyond the unchanging principles grasped by the apocalyptists and insist that God's timing and activity has been uncovered for them in such a way that it is possible to predict the exact time of God's intervention into history and his transformation of it. This has usually resulted in embarrassment and often the obscuring of the continuing message, a message which calls for courageous consistency and which affirms the certainty of God's triumph.

DANIEL AS APOCALYPTIC LITERATURE

Daniel is one of the earliest examples of fully developed apocalyptic literature. The book of Daniel is set in the sixth century B.C. during the Babylonian exile. A large part of its message, however, relates to the tribulations of the Jewish people at the time of the persecutions of Antiochus Epiphanes in the second century B.C.

The book of Daniel naturally divides into two sections. The first six chapters are a series of narratives about the experiences of Daniel and his friends in the court of the pagan kings of the exile. The last six chapters contain reports of four visions of Daniel which symbolically outline history from the Babylonian period onward to the point of God's triumphant intervention into human affairs. The visions dwell at length upon the difficulties of the second century. The narratives exemplify the virtues of courage and faithfulness to the law which were so important during the crises of the second century when the Syrian king, Antiochus Epiphanes, was threatening to obliterate the faithful Jews and their way of life.

There are six narratives and four visions in the book of Daniel, all of which present chapter divisions, except that the last vision includes chapters 10–12. The following is a brief interpretive outline based upon these ten natural sections of the book of Daniel. Before

reading this outline, read straight through Daniel. Then read the
notes below in connection with a more deliberate reading of the
book. (See pp. 99–103 for Dr. Binkley's suggestion about book
study.)

The Virtues of Distinctiveness (chap. 1)

Daniel and his three friends are introduced as faithful Jews who
were captives at the court of King Nebuchadnezzar. Only here are
Daniel and the other three brought together, and the incidents in the
following chapters are related to one another only by the background
provided in chapter 1. The refusal of the three to eat the unclean food
of Nebuchadnezzar, and their success because of it, introduces the
prevailing apocalyptic message that the faithful are to remain consistent in their lives no matter how disadvantageous the circumstances.

The Wisdom of the Faithful (chap. 2)

Nebuchadnezzar had a strange dream which neither he nor his
professional interpreters could understand, a dream in which a mighty
statue represented the empires of history. These empires were sud-
denly shattered and replaced by a new kingdom and a new era. The
significance of this could be perceived only by Daniel, the faithful
servant of God. The wisdom of the world cannot perceive the purposes of God. This insight belongs to the select few.

God's Presence with the Faithful (chap. 3)

As is often true of the faithful, the three friends of Daniel were
asked to compromise their faith by worshiping before an image set up
by Nebuchadnezzar. They refused, indicating that they believed that
God could protect them; but their essential concern was not with their
physical deliverance. Whether God kept them alive or let them die,
they would remain faithful. The apocalyptists recognized the likeli-
hood of suffering and death for many of the faithful, but insisted upon
God's power to keep alive any he chose to preserve.

Human Kings and the Sovereignty of God (chap. 4)

Nebuchadnezzar, king of Babylon, envisioned himself to be the
master of all the earth. His dream and subsequent humiliation by God
demonstrated that the most fearful of human kings and kingdoms
were totally ineffective before the power of the God of Israel.

God's Judgment on Arrogance (chap. 5)

In a grand gesture of contempt for the holy, Belshazzar and his associates used the captured vessels from the Jerusalem Temple as drinking vessels at a riotous party. The story reflects the total disregard for God which often characterized the arrogant confidence of men of great power. Daniel, the man of faith, was able to discern that God does not indefinitely tolerate this arrogance, and the impudent king lost everything as the sources of his power were swept away.

The Testimony of Faithfulness (chap. 6)

The faith of Daniel precipitated conflict even when he sought to mind his own business. Daniel refused to make even a normal compromise in his devotion to the law of God. The apocalyptists believed that any compromise of the faith was a concession to worldly powers, and the faithful man had no recourse but to heed his conscience and trust God without regard for the consequences. The incident illustrates the capacity of God to intervene on behalf of the faithful, but neither the apocalyptists nor the Bible as a whole assume that God will inevitably intervene to prevent martyrdom for one who has remained faithful when challenged by hostile powers.

The Kingdom of the Saints (chap. 7)

The first of the visions has a message very similar to that of the narrative in chapter 2. In the vision, four ugly and grotesque beasts come up out of the sea. (The sea is often symbolic of forces opposing the creating God.) The beasts represent successive earthly kingdoms which stand in opposition to the final rule of God. Each in turn is slain until God sits in judgment and destroys the last one and a new kingdom appears, the kingdom of the saints, which, in contrast to the beasts, is represented by one like a son of man. This anticipation of the establishment of their kingdom sustained the faithful who had to live in the era of the evil kingdoms.

Intervention by God (chap. 8)

Once again the author describes the course of history through the use of animal symbols. As in each of the visions, the writer sees the final time of crisis coming during the Greek period. When the time came for the end of the depravations by the beast, he was destined to be broken by God without human hands. The authors of apocalyptic literature see little human instrumentality in God's control of history.

Approaching Fulfilment (chap. 9)

While confessing the sins of his people, Daniel was visited by the
angel Gabriel. (Angels appear much more frequently in apocalyptic
than other kinds of biblical literature.) The angel assured Daniel that
the time of waiting was approaching an end.

The Time of Trouble and the End of Days (chaps. 10:1 to 12:13)

In the longest of the visions, the recounting of history comes to
its consummation in a description of a time of trouble for those who
are faithful, but at the end of the trouble there is deliverance and even
resurrection for those who have died in their suffering. The moment
of the end was unknown, but its quality was certain.

(For a more lasting impression of the book of Daniel, secure
other commentaries and do further reading on the book of Daniel.)

Revelation as Apocalyptic Literature
Kenneth Wolfe

The book of Revelation deviates from the general pattern of apocalyptic writings in several significant ways. The identity of the author is not concealed. The fact that he identifies himself only as John (1:1,4,9; 22:8) and as one "who . . . was on the island called Patmos on account of the word of God and the testimony of Jesus" (1:9, RSV) indicates that he was well known to those to whom he wrote.

Closely related to the fact that the author identifies himself is the fact that he focuses his attention on those events of his own day. It was customary in other apocalyptic writing to trace events from the present back to the time of the ancient hero in whose name the book was written. The writer of Revelation did not do this. His close identification with the events and people of his time makes more obvious the importance of interpreting his Apocalypse in the light of the historical situation out of which it arose. Evidences from within the book itself point to a time during the reign of the Roman Emperor Domitian (A.D. 81–96) as the setting for the drama which it depicts. It was during this period that the state religion of Rome turned for the first time against the Christians. There had been persecution during the reign of Nero, but that persecution did not grow out of a conflict between the worship of the emperor and the worship of Christ. During the reign of Domitian, the officials of the state religion vigorously promoted the worship of the emperor who took upon himself the title "our Lord and our God."

The cult of the emperor was promoted with special zeal in Asia Minor, the location of the churches which are addressed in the book of Revelation. John described in dramatic and highly symbolic language the conflict which was taking place between the pagan Roman Empire and the church of Jesus Christ. He wrote to encourage the Christian churches to be faithful to their Lord and to assure them that Christ and those who are faithful to him would be victorious.

The book of Revelation also deviates from the normal literary style of apocalyptic literature. After the description of the opening

Dr. Wolfe is associate professor of New Testament Interpretation and Greek, Midwestern Baptist Theological Seminary, Kansas City, Missouri.

vision of Christ (1:9–20), a common feature of apocalyptic literature, there follow (chaps. 2–3) seven letters written in direct episto-
lary style to seven churches in Asia Minor. These letters reflect a
close personal knowledge of both the churches addressed and their
environment. The book also closes like an epistle (22:21).

The interpretative outline which follows seeks to describe only
that part of the book of Revelation which contains the Apocalypse
itself, 4:1 to 22:5.

The sovereign Lord of history (4:1 to 5:14).—The Apocalypse
of John begins with a scene which portrays God on his throne with a
scroll sealed with seven seals in his hand and the Lamb, who was
slain but has become victorious, who is the only one worthy to open
the scroll. This first scene introduces the new basis upon which
Christian apocalyptic literature is built, the redeeming act of God in
Jesus. The victory which has been wrought in him foretokens the final
victory over evil and the forces of evil.

Prelude to judgment—the seven seals (6:1 to 8:1).—The second scene of the drama foretells the judgment which the Lord of
history will visit upon the forces of evil. Warfare, the calamities that
follow in the wake of war, and natural disasters are described in
symbolic language. Before the breaking of the seventh seal, there is
an interlude in which 144,000 from the tribes of Israel and a "great
multitude," which probably symbolizes the redeemed from among the
Gentiles, are sealed. The sealing most likely symbolizes divine protection against the plagues to be visited upon the peoples of the earth.

Preparation for judgment—the seven trumpets (8:2 to
11:19).—The woes of the seven trumpets are essentially the same as
those of the seven seals arranged in a different order and presented
through different symbols.

Interruption of the three series of seven (12:1 to 14:20).—In
this scene a woman appears in heaven in birth pains, threatened by a
dragon who in turn is overthrown by Michael. The dragon pursues
the woman to earth where two beasts appear. The child is undoubtedly Christ, the first beast imperial Rome; and the second beast is
probably the imperial priesthood which compelled the people to
worship the emperor. After a vision of the Lamb and the 144,000,
there is an announcement of judgment upon Babylon (Rome).

Divine judgment executed—the seven bowls (15:1 to
16:21).—The plagues which befall the earth at the pouring out of

the seven bowls very closely parallel those which followed the blow-
ing of the seven trumpets. John did not present a chronological
succession of eschatological events. He seems to set forth the judgment which is to befall the enemies of God and of the church in 6:1
to 8:1. Then there is a preparation for the execution of that judgment
which covers some of the same ground as 8:2 to 14:20. Finally, there
is the presentation of the judgment and that which is to follow upon
the judgment in 15:1 to 22:6.

The fall of Babylon (17:1 to 19:10).—The seer, John, is shown
the judgment of the harlot Babylon (Rome). In the ensuing scenes
kings, merchants, and seafarers mourn the fall of Rome while the
hosts of heaven rejoice and praise God for his righteous judgment.

Final victory (19:11 to 22:5).—The final scene of the drama
presents the victory of Christ over the antichrist, the thousand year
interim kingdom, the final judgment, and the new Jerusalem. This
section poses the difficult question, debated from the second century
to the present, of the extent to which the coming events portrayed
here, along with earthly millennium, can be harmonized with the
remainder of the New Testament.

Interpreting Prophetic Literature
Roy Honeycutt

Despite many commendable and frequent efforts to "learn the Bible" or to "teach the Bible," there is a sense in which the Bible can be neither learned nor taught. Ultimately, the Bible can only be experienced; and the reader must be drawn into its unfolding action as a participant rather than as a spectator before it speaks with living power to his life situation. In this regard, the observation of Northrop Frye concerning literature generally is equally applicable to the Bible: "The difficulty often felt in 'teaching literature' arises from the fact that it cannot be done: the criticism of literature is all that can be directly taught." [1] You may learn how better to appreciate literature, and you may master the techniques of literary criticism; but you must ultimately experience with the writer the pathos or joy, the comedy or tragedy, which is conveyed in literary form.

The Bible must be experienced as the words "come alive" in one's present moment of confrontation. Principles of interpretation may be taught and factual material drawn from the Bible, and the biblical revelation still may not have been shared. *For understanding the revelation involves a personal meeting between the individual and the Lord, precipitated by the Bible, medium of revelation—an experience reflected in the words of the hymn, "Beyond the sacred page I seek Thee, Lord."*

Perhaps one reason some are unmoved by the Scriptures is the all too common failure to recognize that one cannot "learn the Bible." One can only *learn* principles of interpretation and stylistic analysis which will equip him to experience the Bible, to re-create and then live within the life situation portrayed within its pages.

Techniques of interpretation may be well illustrated by considering a prophetic book brief enough to be examined in detail, yet inclusive enough to provide illustrative examples which will clarify principles of interpretation. The book of Habakkuk is a greatly neglected book for many people, yet it has a significant message. This message is conveyed through a variety of literary forms which in turn

---

[1] Northrop Frye, *Fables of Identity* (New York: Harcourt, Brace & World, Inc., 1963), p. 7.

Dr. Honeycutt is professor of Old Testament Interpretation and Hebrew, Midwestern Baptist Theological Seminary, Kansas City, Missouri.

reflect several stylistic characteristics common to prophetic literature. An understanding of Habakkuk might involve the following procedures.

First, begin by reading the book through in its entirety several times, preferably using as wide a variety of translations as possible.

Second, look in a good one-volume commentary for the date and historical circumstances of the prophet, as well as the general theme(s) of the book. Habakkuk, for example, was written in the late seventh century B.C. and was set against the background of national oppression (probably by the Babylonians), as well as the faithlessness of men within Judah. The central purpose of Habakkuk is the attempt to reconcile the violence of the age with the sovereignty of a moral and just God—how can God permit violence and injustice? To the prophet, as to many in this generation, it seems as though God does nothing to counteract the irresponsible violence of the age.

Third, since the book cannot be reduced to a single idea, it is necessary to separate it into a limited number of major concepts which may in turn be subdivided into emphases within the major blocks of material. Prophets probably originally spoke their messages in quite brief, pithy forms which were later collected and, through editing by the prophet or a prophetic disciple, were arranged in larger blocks of material. It is imperative that one seek to determine the methodology used by editors of prophetic material in arranging the original utterances of the prophet. What are some of the editorial techniques used by the editors of prophetic material?

Editors of prophetic material often used *catchwords,* introducing separate sections of material with the same word. (See "Woe," Hab. 2:6,9,12,15,19.) Often the *small words,* conjunctions and prepositions, are ignored by the casual reader of the Bible. Yet, these are frequently used to introduce the conclusion to an argument. (See Hab. 1:4, *"So* the law is slacked. . . . *For* the wicked surround the righteous"; Isa. 45:3–6, *"that* you may know . . . *for* the sake of my servant . . . *that* men may know.") Often a key word is repeated. For example, the editor used the same word (*'ur,* to awake) three times in Isaiah 51:9,17; 52:1, and by so doing suggests a proper division of material, as well as the collection of all three divisions within one heading (Isa. 51:9 to 52:12).

The *question and answer method* is often used in prophetic material and is a major motif in Habakkuk (see 1:2,5,12; 2:1–2).

Or, conversation between the prophet and the Lord, or the people, often forms a natural division; and one should watch for a change of person in subdividing the major motifs. In addition, there are other prophetic literary forms which cannot be considered separately: the *lawsuit motif* in which the Lord brings his people to "court" (Mic. 6:1–2); the *argumentative form* in which the prophetic message is cast in the form of a debate between the Lord and the people (Isa. 1:2–26); *biographical narratives* (Isa. 7:1 to 8:15); *predictions* (Amos 9:11–15); *oracular poems* (Amos 1:3 to 2:16; 4:6–12); *indictments* (Isa. 1:18–20); *mourning songs* (Amos 5:1–2); *laments* (Hos. 6:1–3; 14:3–4); *sermons* (Ezek. 20); *mocking songs* (Isa. 37:22–29); and other brief literary forms. These should be recognized and treated as separate emphases within the subsidiary thrust of the prophetic book. The longest and most distinct illustration of this in Habakkuk is the psalm which appears in the third chapter. In isolating the major themes of Habakkuk, one should obviously treat the psalm as a separate major division within the book.

The paragraph division in the Revised Standard Version is also a helpful guide for isolating subsidiary emphases within larger units of material. Although these divisions are not infallible, they do follow very ancient divisions in the Hebrew text and almost invariably collect single concepts or ideas within the paragraph. Very seldom will the Bible student find it appropriate to break the paragraph division within the Revised Standard Version.

Assuming that you have examined the historical background of the book, understanding to some degree the international, moral, social, and spiritual conditions of the late seventh century, how can you best proceed in isolating the major themes of the book? The question and answer motif suggests that chapter 1 should be treated as a distinct, major emphasis. The fact that the third chapter is a psalm (3:1,9,19) indicates that it should be treated separately. The second chapter remains as another major division, for it contains the vision (2:1–5) plus the lengthy section which the editor (whether the prophet or another) has arranged under the fivefold use of "woe" (2:6–20). Each of these three major sections may then be subdivided into subsidiary emphases.

In this manner you will hopefully arrive at that point where the life situation of Habakkuk has been so reconstructed that you may then experience with the prophet his agony and turmoil produced by his conviction that despite the enormity of the violence and lawlessness of his age God was doing nothing. Through successive lines of discourse and argument, you may experience with Habakkuk the unfolding revelation that God is at work, and that one should learn to develop particular attitudes toward life as he awaits the fulfilment of God's purposes. By this feeling of empathy, you will experience the re-created crises and consolations which characterized the life of the prophet. But of this you may be sure, until you have experienced the prophetic book with the prophet, you will fail to enter fully into the revelation of God mediated through the book.

Although the following interpretative outline makes no claim to finality, it does represent the writer's understanding of the experience which you may have in reading the book of Habakkuk.

God for a Violent Age
An Interpretative Outline of Habakkuk

Part One: Questioning God—The Presence of Evil and the Action of God, 1:1–17

I. When God Does Nothing (1:1–4)
 1. Questions from a religious perspective (1:1–3)
  (1) The first question: "O Lord, how long. . . ?" The question suggests an anguish common to man, an accusation often made, and the absence of divine action.
  (2) The second question: "O Lord, why. . . ?" Both the reality and the reasons for violence are graphically portrayed.
 2. Consequences of unchecked violence (1:4)

II. Who Would Believe It? (1:5–11)
 1. The wonder of God's action (1:5; note "for")
  Contrary to the prophet's conviction that God was doing nothing in his age, he was at work in the context of strife and violence.
 2. The way of God's action (1:6–11; note "for")
  God is using the turbulent forces of history in the fulfilment of his ultimate purposes.

III. How Could God Use Him? (1:12–17)
 1. The nature of God suggests that he cannot use the people earlier described (1:12–13b, note the question).
 2. The prophet's question—Is this immoral nation (Babylon,

probably) not only to be used by God, but left unchecked in the world? (1:13b–17, see the affirmation followed by the question.)

Part Two: Man's Attitude in Life's Crises (2:1–20)
What does man need in the face of crises, an answer or an attitude? Attitudes, not answers, undergird human personality in the midst of crises.

I. Learning Patience and Purpose (2:1–3)
  1. The certitude of faith—laying one's problem before the Lord (2:1).
  2. The clarity of revelation—make it so plain that "he may run who reads it" (2:2, RSV).
  3. The consummation of God's purposes, waiting on God, "If it seem slow, wait for it" (2:3, RSV).
II. Living with integrity (2:4–5, this is probably the "vision" of vv. 2–3)
  1. The inevitable failure of the man whose "soul is not upright" (2:4, RSV).
  2. The responsibility of the righteous to live by (in) his faith (i.e., faithfulness)—even if one cannot alter national faithlessness, one may live with personal faithfulness (2:4b, see "but," for contrast).
  3. The instability of the arrogant man stands in contrast with the righteous (2:5, see "moreover").
III. The Inevitable Doom of Evil (2:6–20, note recurring use of "woe")
  Although such awareness does not answer that problem of evil, one should recognize that evil carries within itself the seeds of its own destruction.
  1. Oppressed people inevitably rise against the oppressor (2:6–8).
  2. Exaltation at the expense of others forfeits the "life" of the oppressor (2:9–11).
  3. Godless advancement brings no ultimate satisfaction; it shall be destroyed (2:12–14).
  4. Destruction of the dignity and rights of another precipitates a kindred fate (2:15–17).
  5. Substitutes for God (idolatry) are best characterized as sheer folly (2:18–19).

Part Three: Trusting God (3:1–19)

Chapter 3 is a psalm in which the redemptive power of the Lord is central. The essential characteristic of the psalm is the confidence and transformation of life one may experience through the redeeming Lord.

I. Trusting God to Renew His Revelation (3:1–15)
1. The renewal of God's redemptive action constitutes man's abiding hope (3:1–2).
   (1) The memory of God's mighty acts has been preserved, and in turn preserves (3:1–2a).
   (2) Prayer for the continuation of the Lord's revelation, with a plea for wrath tempered with mercy (3:2b).
2. Remembrance and recitation of the Lord's redemptive activity from another generation, probably the Exodus (3:3–15).
   This passage demands a sense of poetic appreciation in discerning the revelation of God.

II. Transformation Through Trusting God (3:16–19, the response "I hear . . ." introduces a new nation)
1. The awe-inspiring remembrance of the Lord's redemptive action startles the prophet (3:16a).
2. Patience is created whereby the prophet waits for God to act (3:16b, see Isa. 30:15 on quietness and trust).
3. A willingness to rejoice in God despite adversity replaces the skepticism of the prophet (3:17–18).
4. Reliance upon God as his strength has replaced personal self-confidence (3:19).

Studying the Miracles of Jesus
George Thomason

No man is a number, a type, or a picture on the wall. A man, any man, is a three-dimensional figure living among certain people, within a definite stage of history, and moving about upon a specific plot of the earth's surface. This is especially true of Jesus. He was not only God walking the dusty roads of Galilee. He was not just a simple Galilean peasant. This most complex of all men was both the unique Son of God and a Jew of the first century. Even to partly understand him, we must see him in his earthly setting. And our interest should be not only in what he said, but in what he did. To deny that unusual deeds accompanied his life is the height of futility. To try really to see those deeds—his miracles—and understand them, let us ask seven questions, using this method as a technique to enrich historical understanding. After the questions have been amplified, they will then be applied to John 2:1–11: "The Water into Wine."

I. The Questions

1. What did the miracle mean to those who first experienced and observed it?
2. What did the miracle mean to Jesus' disciples who had given their lives to him in discipleship?
3. Since the theology of the first disciples was derived from their Bible, the Old Testament, what does the Old Testament teach about miracles?
4. Even more pointedly, what does the Old Testament teach about miracles in relationship to the Messiah?
5. How did the religious parties of Jesus' day interpret the Old Testament on the question of Messiah and miracles?
6. From the New Testament account, what did Jesus himself think about the miracles?
7. Where in the ministry of Jesus does the specific miracle come?

II. Questions Amplified

1. What did the miracle mean to those who first experienced and observed it?

Dr. Thomason is professor of New Testament Interpretation and Greek, Midwestern Baptist Theological Seminary, Kansas City, Missouri.

This question is the beginning effort to place the event back in its first-century setting. Immediately, however, it raises the question of that age's credibility of miracles in general. Some have called the first century an age of miracles, meaning thereby that people were expecting miracles. Those who thus characterize that age would strongly contrast it with the modern scientific era. On the other hand, one of the problems of the modern scientific era is its tendency to egotism—sometimes assuming that all preceding it were ignorant and unlearned. In the Gospel account of the miracles, the people were as impressed by them as any modern man would be. Any observant man of any age knows how nature ordinarily operates. Since Christianity became established on the basis that it was accompanied by unusual events, the policy of assuming miracles and trying to understand them would be better than asking whether or not they actually happened. Instead of the interpreter of the New Testament consuming much of his time, energy, brain cells, and soul power on, "Did the miracles happen?" he should ask, "What did they mean?"

2. What did the miracle mean to the disciples?

When this question is presented, some might raise the problem of the historical accuracy of the New Testament. True enough, the New Testament was written by the disciples of Jesus. Also obvious is the contention that the New Testament is not objective history but the inspired record of the preaching of convinced men who were trying to win other men. However, their sense of urgency should not be used to disprove the truthfulness of their preaching. A man can be both earnest and honest. The Gospel of John frankly admits (21:25) that the New Testament does not record all that Jesus said and did. It does tell what the disciples saw in him, at least that part of their experience and observation which they felt, under God's leadership, would be necessary to communicate the gospel. Quite vital, therefore, is the question of what the disciples saw in the miracles, at least as far as it can be dealt with in the written record.

3. What does the Old Testament teach about miracles?

The modern Christian, at least in the educational setting, cannot imagine himself without a Bible—a Bible composed of both the Old and New Testaments. No time machine can take the modern Christian out of his own setting into an earlier age, but the effort must be made. And when the effort is made, the realization will come that the Bible of the original disciples was what we call the Old Testament.

The basic message of the Old Testament is that of the God who delivered Israel from Egypt. With a mighty arm, he broke the will of Pharaoh and brought his people across the sea, into the desert, and finally into the Promised Land itself. This deliverance was marked by some unusual events such as the plagues, the crossing of the sea, and the preservation of God's people in the desert. The faith of Israel was in a God who did things, sometimes in unusual ways. *To the Jew of Jesus' day therefore, a miracle was an act of God, a visible act of God performed on behalf of his people.*

The miracles of the Old Testament are identified with the revelation of God. Moses identified himself as the representative of God by the miracle of the staff and the leprous hand. The prophets had their special signs, sometimes miraculous and sometimes not; but when they were regarded as miraculous the people felt God had spoken. The illustration of Nicodemus may be used as characteristic of the people of Jesus' day; to him the signs indicated the presence of God in a special way. (See John 3:2.)

4. What does the Old Testament teach about miracles in relationship to the Messiah?

The book of Isaiah presents a future golden age which is identified with the Chosen One of God, or the special Servant of God. During this predicted golden age, man's weaknesses were to be rectified and hopes realized by God's intervention into human society in a special way, such as by the use of miracles. Many things from the life of Jesus confirm this truth, but two are especially significant. One of these is the sermon of Jesus in the synagogue at Nazareth which is given in Luke 4. " 'He has sent me to proclaim release to the captives and recovering of sight to the blind" (RSV).

The other event is the occasion when John the Baptist sent disciples inquiring of Jesus whether he was the one who should come. "Jesus answered them, 'Go and tell John what you hear and see: the blind receive their sight and the lame walk, lepers are cleansed and the deaf hear, and the dead are raised up, and the poor have good news preached to them' " (Matt. 11:4–5, RSV). This verse is taken from Isaiah 35:5–6; 61:1.

The conclusion can be drawn that the miracles of Jesus were themselves the fulfilment of the prophecy of the Old Testament concerning the coming age, and one of the major signs that the age or kingdom of God had arrived. These miracles, in addition to confirm-

ing the arrival of the Messiah and his kingdom, also are descriptive of
the nature of the Messiah and his kingdom.

5. How did the religious parties of Jesus' day interpret the Old
   Testament on the question of Messiah and miracles?

Many scholars feel that most of the Jews of the first century had
a limited concept of the Messiah, and that they certainly had no
concept concerning any miracles relating to that Messiah. The limited
material that is available relating to the Pharisees would indicate that
their expectancy concerning the Messiah did not involve an anticipation of the miraculous. One existing nonbiblical work from the period
between the Testaments is concerned in matters of Messiah only with
a Son of David who will rule in righteousness over the nations. No
mention of the miraculous is made at all.

The case is different with the people of the time of the Dead Sea
scrolls. Other Jews may not have associated Isaiah and his golden age
with the Messiah, but the Scroll people most certainly did. Their main
purpose in withdrawing to the desert was to await the Messiah, and
their favorite study in waiting was Isaiah. However, it would seem
that, though they saw the messianic age as an age of miracles, they
did not necessarily see the Messiah himself as a miracle worker. Also,
their concept of Messiah would seem to be a multiple figure, rather
than a single person, including a prophet like Moses, a prince like
David, and a priest like Aaron. Differences existed between the
Scrolls and the New Testament, but the Scroll people also saw as
messianic those passages from Isaiah that Jesus and John the Baptist
used.

6. From the New Testament account, what did Jesus himself
   think about the miracles?

Jesus saw the miracles as a demonstration that the golden age of
the Messiah had arrived. "If it is by the finger of God that I cast out
demons, then the kingdom of God has come upon you" (Luke 11:20,
RSV). The sermon at Nazareth already discussed would help to
confirm this truth.

However, the miracles did evoke deep concern on the part of
Jesus. In the temptation experience, Jesus was dealing with the
problem of how to direct unusual power. Was his problem the kind of
miracle or just any miracle at all? Throughout his ministry he, at
times, seemed embarrassed by the miracles and would strenuously
demand the people he had helped to keep silent. The most likely

answer is that Jesus would always keep the moral and ethical element uppermost in his ministry; he would always insist that the miracle remain a servant to the messianic mission.

7. At what point of development in the ministry of Jesus does a specific miracle come?

The Gospel accounts indicate that Jesus worked diligently to teach his disciples some basic truths about his own mission as Messiah and about the Messiah's kingdom. His teaching, in words and deeds, was directed toward that development. Since such is the case, the possibility is very real that a certain miracle might be fitting at one point in his ministry and unsuited in another.

Jesus was always dedicated to the Father's will; but experience, the Old Testament Scriptures, and the presence of the Father helped to lead him into the full meaning of that will. From the human standpoint, the miracles would also be a part of his own developing experience.

III. Application: The Water into Wine

Many have been disturbed over John 2:1–11. Persons at one end of the theological spectrum are upset because of the magnitude of the miracle. At the other end, there are those who are disturbed by this miracle because of their feelings about the use of wine as a beverage. Neither group is facing the real issue: What did the miracle mean? What was Jesus trying to do through the event?

The passage states plainly that this miracle was to develop the faith of the new disciples. "This, the first of his signs, Jesus did at Cana in Galilee, and manifested his glory; and his disciples believed in him" (2:11, RSV). This miracle was not for the general public at all, but was to aid these men in becoming acquainted with Jesus—who he was and what he had come to do.

What does the Old Testament say about wine? When they were talking about wine, most of the prophets denounced drunkenness in no uncertain terms. The proponent of temperance can be assured that the prophets, and Jesus, did not encourage the wrong use of earth's bounties.

But the prophets did connect wine and the golden age. Note Isaiah 62:8: "The Lord has sworn by his right hand and by his mighty arm: 'I will not again give your grain to be food for your enemies, and foreigners shall not drink your wine for which you have labored: but those who garner it shall eat it and praise the Lord, and those who gather it shall drink it in the courts of my sanctuary' " (RSV).

Both Joel and Amos were strong ethical preachers, and both spoke about the great age to come. Note these words from Joel: "The threshing floors shall be full of grain, the vats shall overflow with wine and oil" (Joel 2:24, RSV).

Joel 3:18 is even more relevant. "And in that day the mountains shall drip sweet wine, and the hills shall flow with milk, and all the stream beds of Judah shall flow with water" (RSV).

The above passages were a part of the Scroll people's texts on the age of Messiah. We do not know how literal that expected fulfilment was to be, for the statements seem to be in the form of symbol and hyperbole. But what better way could there be to develop the faith of new disciples than to make a known symbol a reality? Immature men often need such a sign if their small faith is to grow.

What did Jesus himself think about the miracle of the water into wine? At the beginning when Mary came to him with the request, there seemed to be some hesitancy on his part. Prior to this time he had considered turning stones into bread and had rejected the action as an unworthy one. Some interpreters have felt that turning water into wine was unworthy as well. It might seem that opening blind eyes, healing lepers, and straightening crooked limbs would have been a better first miracle than the luxury of a large supply of wine.

But the occasion was a real need in a genuine historical setting. The couple getting married, probably poor, had had their comparatively meager resources exhausted. Every miracle comes in a living, true to life setting of people with problems. Just to turn water into wine, without a need, would have been a stunt, the kind of thing Jesus steadfastly refused to do.

Even so, men have needs much more serious than being able to show complete hospitality to their guests. Did Jesus have any other motivation? It must be remembered that his early ministry was performed against the background and, to some degree, within a strong pattern of asceticism. John the Baptist was a rigid ascetic, refraining from the use of wine and practically everything else.

Was Christianity to be a life of fulness or asceticism? Since people would already be associating Jesus with John the Baptist, he had to do something that would show that he was God's chosen one for the golden age, that the life of his followers was to be lived in the midst of men rather than separate from them. That Jesus saw the wedding feast as being the outstanding symbol of life's fulness, in contrast to asceticism, can be demonstrated by his own statement. When the Pharisees asked him why his disciples did not fast as John's had done, Jesus replied: " 'Can you make wedding guests fast while the bridegroom is with them?' " (Luke 5:34, RSV). It is highly probable that Jesus felt that the best way to separate himself from John and put himself within the mainstream of the life of his people was to perform a miracle at a wedding feast.

Summary

Jesus turned water into wine as his first miracle to teach that he would meet men's problems where they were. The golden age of the prophets had now come. Jesus showed that Christianity offers the abundant life rather than asceticism. Above all, this miracle was a sign which helped to develop the faith of the first disciples that Jesus was Messiah.

Suggested Reading on the Miracles
1. Bible Dictionaries
   The Interpreter's Dictionary of the Bible (New York: Abingdon Press, 1962).
   K. Stendahl, "Biblical Theology, Contemporary," Vol. 1, pp. 418–32.
   O. Betz, "Dead Sea Scrolls," Vol. 1, pp. 790–802.
   K. Grobel, "Interpretation, History and Principles Of," Vol. 2, pp. 718–24.
   The New Bible Dictionary (Grand Rapids: William B. Eerdmans Publishing Co., 1962).
   F. F. Bruce, "Dead Sea Scrolls," p. 299.
   F. F. Bruce, "Interpretation, Biblical," pp. 566–68.
   M. H. Cressey, "Miracles," pp. 828–31.
2. Commentaries
   Charles R. Erdman, *Commentaries on the New Testament* (Philadelphia: The Westminister Press, 1936).
3. Books
   G. Ernest Wright, *God Who Acts* (London: SCM Press LTD, 1952).
   David A. Redding, *The Miracles of Christ* (Westwood, N. J.: Fleming H. Revell, 1964).

CHAPTER FOUR

Guidelines for
Effective
Bible Study

There is something in the Bible of supreme worth to our lives which is to be found nowhere else. Using the tools of biblical scholarship, the message of the Bible can be studied effectively in the English language. An understanding of some basic principles of biblical interpretation, as set out in the preceding chapter, assists in Bible study.

Now it is important that we consider a plan of Bible study. The plan set forth in this chapter is an adaptable method. It can be used by anyone who desires to establish a long-range plan of biblical studies. It can be used by individuals or groups who wish to restudy the Bible with the assistance of a carefully selected set of tools prepared by biblical scholars and with close attention to what God is saying to us today through the Bible.

The plan offered is definite but flexible. The rapid reading of the Bible as a whole, for example, can be omitted by persons who are already acquainted with the arrangement of the biblical literature and who have decided what parts of the Bible they want to study intensively. However, each of the guidelines should be considered carefully. For we are concerned in this chapter with the formation of a lifelong habit of Bible study which will meet the tests of scholarly integrity and practical effectiveness.

Across the decades this writer has conferred with hundreds of students who were in academic difficulty. Frequently I have heard a student say, "I do not know how to study"; and in most instances the student was telling the truth. Many factors are involved in academic failure, but three are outstanding: (1) doubt about the value of the study for the achievement of the student's purpose of life; (2) lack of a clear understanding of the methodology essential to a mastery of the subject matter under consideration; (3) failure to give adequate time, attention, and energy to the study each day or each week.

These factors are associated, also, with the low level of biblical knowledge in the United States today. An enormous number of persons are not convinced that the message of the Bible is important, that appropriate methods of biblical study can be developed, or that effective Bible study merits and requires high priority in the rigorous schedules of contemporary society.

There is in the mainstream of American Christianity the strong conviction that every man has an unconditional right to read the Bible and to respond to God's message. This book has been prepared out of a conviction that the hour has come for intelligent laymen in the churches, as well as for devout ministers and biblical scholars, to exercise this right and to assume this responsibility.

We draw attention to some guidelines for persons who plan to read the Bible with understanding and to use its insights effectively. (See bold type for a summary of guidelines.)

Decide to Study

The first requirement is a personal decision to undertake a systematic and thorough study of the Bible. Although portions of the Bible are easily understood by children, an orderly and thoroughgoing study of the Scriptures, including such profound documents as the book of Job and the letter to the Romans, demands the best efforts of mature minds.

In this task, the average Christian is not to be intimidated by the learning and the language of the biblical scholars. Instead, we are to employ the tools produced by their labor in an effort to understand God's mighty acts in the history of his people and the revelation of his redemptive purpose in the mission and message of Jesus Christ. We are to "read, mark, learn, and inwardly digest" the structure and substance of the books of the Bible. In this endeavor, we are not to be deflected by the false assumptions that the message of the Bible is too remote to influence daily living, that it is too familiar to be interesting, and that it is too obscure to be understood. We are to examine the message of the Bible with the assurance that it can be understood and that its message can give practical guidance. (See pp. 117–20 for a long and thorough plan of Bible reading recommended by the American Bible Society.)

If our study of the Bible is to be systematic and thorough, not fragmentary and superficial, it will be necessary for us to include it as an important item in our schedule. A busy physician opened his book of appointments with the comment, "Let me consult my mind." A schedule is not "a mind," but many of us actually live not only by faith but also by schedule. Unless we include a definite time for Bible study in the schedule, the study will not be done or it will be done occasionally and superficially.

Bible reading can be as firmly established in our schedule as the reading of the newspaper. During the hard days of World War II, a man in a responsible position decided to read a part of the Bible each morning before he looked at the newspaper. His first thoughts at the beginning of the day were of God and his message to men. He rediscovered things he had forgotten about the strength of men and of nations and became a more adequate interpreter of the message of the Bible and of momentous events in contemporary life.

Engage in a Rapid Reading of the Bible as a Whole

In spite of the fact that many thoughtful and conscientious people have bogged down in the process, one way to secure an adequate introduction to the whole drama set forth in the Old and New Testaments is to *read the Bible in its entirety*. If this is done with a clear understanding of the objectives to be achieved, it will not be an ordeal. Instead, it will be an instructive and enjoyable experience.

There are more than twelve hundred pages in an average edition of the Bible. If you will undertake to read one hundred pages per week, you can complete the preliminary reading within approximately thirteen weeks. This is not the type or amount of reading you would select for a brief morning or evening devotional period. It would be necessary for you to set aside a definite daily study period for the purpose of doing this quick reading of the Bible.

The objectives of this rapid reading are (1) to gain firsthand knowledge of the arrangement of materials and structure of thought; (2) to discern the types of literature; (3) to identify key words;

(4) to get acquainted with outstanding personalities; (5) to discover central themes; and (6) to select books of the Bible for further study. This is not a very difficult task, but it will test the strength of your decision to make a systematic and thorough study of the Bible.

Review what is said about the tools of biblical scholarship in chapter 2. Select the version of the Bible you will use in the reading of the Bible as a whole. If feasible, purchase an appropriate concordance, dictionary of the Bible, and the Bible atlas.

Before you begin this extensive reading of the Bible, purchase a loose-leaf notebook and write each of the following topics at the top of a separate page: Key Words, Outstanding Personalities, Central Themes, Books of the Bible, Quotations, and Questions. Then, as you read with pen or pencil in hand, list in your notebook the words, personalities, themes, and books of the Bible which you plan to study intensively later. Copy accurately the quotations from the Bible which you intend to remember. It is very important also to write in your notebook the questions which come to your mind as you read the Bible. These questions will become a vital part of the learning process as you ponder them in your mind and as you search for answers. This preliminary work is a simple procedure; but if it is done honestly and intelligently, it will be valuable. It will be a record of your response to the primary documents of the Christian faith and a foundation for long-range study. (See p. 107 for a sample notebook entry.)

The books of the Bible are not arranged in chronological order, and it is difficult to determine the most desirable sequence in which to read them. It seems wise to begin the reading of the Bible with Jesus as presented in the Gospels. Then read the Old Testament as a manifestation of God's purpose in the history of his people and as preparation for the coming of Jesus into the world. Finally, read the remainder of the New Testament in the perspective of the message and mission of Jesus Christ.

We recommend, therefore, that you read the books of the Bible in the sequence outlined here.

Read **the Gospels** in the following order: Mark, Matthew, Luke, John

Read the books of the Old Testament in the order of the Hebrew Bible:

The Law: Genesis, Exodus, Leviticus, Numbers, Deuteronomy

The Prophets: Joshua, Judges, 1 and 2 Samuel, 1 and 2 Kings, Isaiah, Jeremiah, Ezekiel, Hosea, Joel, Amos, Obadiah, Jonah,

Micah, Nahum, Habakkuk, Zephaniah, Haggai, Zechariah, Malachi

The Writings: Psalms, Proverbs, Job, Ruth, The Song of Solomon, Lamentations, Ecclesiastes, Esther, Daniel, Ezra-Nehemiah, 1 and 2 Chronicles

Read the **other books of the New Testament** in the following order: The Acts of the Apostles

The Letters: Romans, 1 and 2 Corinthians, Galatians, Ephesians, Philippians, Colossians, 1 and 2 Thessalonians, 1 and 2 Timothy, Titus, Philemon, Hebrews, James, 1 and 2 Peter, 1, 2, and 3 John, Jude

The Revelation of John

(See p. 106 for a chart of this Bible-reading plan.)

At the heart of the Bible is the supreme revelation of God's redemptive purpose in Jesus Christ. It may be helpful to begin the reading of the Gospel of Mark with four questions in mind: (1) *What kind of person was Jesus?* (2) *What did he say and do?* (3) *What was he seeking to accomplish?* (4) *What does he mean to me?*

Study Key Words of the Bible

Another approach to Bible study is to engage in a search for an understanding of the words of the Bible. The purpose of such a search is to learn as precisely and comprehensively as possible what the biblical writers really meant by the words they used.

In all languages the old words are exceptionally difficult to define. The old words are frequently short words, such as "life," "light," "love," and "truth." In dealing with these old and elemental words, two questions are to be answered: What does the word mean? What is the *total* meaning of the word?

In the study of the words of the Bible, a knowledge of Hebrew and Greek is valuable. Such knowledge enables a biblical scholar to trace the history and meaning of a word through the Old and New Testaments in the original languages and to make full use of the technical language used in the most scholarly commentaries. However, we do not have to have knowledge of Greek and Hebrew because we have excellent translations of the Old and New Testaments into the English language.

There are at least four procedures that can be used in the study of the great biblical words.

Study words which you select as key words based on your own

reading of the Bible.—You will find understanding and joy in the exploration of what these words meant to the biblical writers who used them.

Use a concordance to locate the passages in the Bible where the word under consideration is used.—For example, the passages in which the word "disciples" appears in the Revised Standard Version are listed in *Nelson's Complete Concordance of the Revised Standard Version Bible.* Note that the word is used only once in the Old Testament but very frequently in the New Testament. Notice also that in the New Testament the word is used in the four Gospels and in Acts. A study of this word as used in the New Testament will clarify the relationship between Jesus and his disciples and provide insight into his work as a teacher.

Read the definition and discussion of the meaning of the word in a good Bible dictionary or theological word book.—(See annotated bibliography, pp. 136–41, for suggestions.)

Study the specific passages in which the word is used in the Bible.—The word is united with other words in phrases, sentences, and paragraphs to express thought and action. For example, study the word "disciples" in Luke 6:13: "And when it was day, he called his disciples, and chose from them twelve, whom he named apostles" (RSV). Read the exposition of this passage in whatever commentaries are available to you.

After you have studied the word "disciples" in each passage in which it is used in the New Testament, write a summary of your understanding of the subject "Disciples of Jesus." What you write will be your own work based upon your study of the primary source in English.

These four procedures can be used in an intensive study of such biblical words as faith, fellowship, forgiveness, justice, love, reconciliation, sin, salvation, truth, and wisdom.

The study of the great words of the Bible is essential to a deep and growing knowledge of biblical truth. Such a study enables us to act wisely in regard to the moral and religious dimensions of vital issues in our time. (See pp. 113–17 for a further study of words.)

Study the Outstanding Personalities of the Bible

There is a wealth of biographical material in the Old and New Testaments. In your rapid reading of this material, you will discover the biblical personalities in whom you are most interested. In the months and years ahead, you will be able to study at least a few of these biblical characters and to learn what God said through them to their generation and what he is saying through them to us.

For the kind of serious study we are recommending, it will probably be advisable to concentrate upon two or three of the great personalities of the Old Testament, such as David, Isaiah, Jeremiah, Amos, and Hosea; and two or three of the major characters in the New Testament, such as Paul, John, Peter, Luke, and James. In any event, do not fail to study the words and deeds of Jesus Christ, whose life on earth helps us to understand and appreciate the nature and destiny of man.

One of the dynamic and unforgettable personalities of the Old Testament is David. A brief consideration of his life and work will illustrate the procedures involved in a thorough study of a biblical character.

Study the total message of the Bible concerning David.—This will require hard work, but it will place the study on the solid basis of the primary sources in English. There is a vast amount of material about David in the Bible. It includes about one thousand references in the Old Testament and sixty references in the New. This body of knowledge concerning an ancient leader merits the most careful examination and contains an authentic message for modern man.

Identify the crucial decisions made by David throughout his career.—The purpose of his life, the strength and weakness of his character, the quality of his mind, and the power of his religious faith are reflected in the decisions he made as a young man, as a mature man, and as an old man.

See clearly the tasks to which he devoted his intelligence and energy.—He was a political and military leader. He was a poet and a musician. He was a wise and resourceful administrator in the area of public affairs. He was genuinely interested in religious faith and religious institutions.

Determine what qualities were deeply characteristic of David as a person and as a leader.—He had a rare combination of kindness and cruelty. The kindness is seen in his magnificent friendship with Jonathan. The cruelty is expressed in the destruction of Uriah whose wife he had stolen. He was exceptionally courageous and participated in the struggle for security for himself and for his people. Israel became a powerful nation under his leadership. He possessed the insight of a poet and the skill of a musician, but he failed to maintain discipline and honor in his own family. He exercised undisputed authority from Egypt to the Euphrates, but he did not have the moral strength to control personal passion when he saw Bathsheba taking a bath. His religious faith was inadequately related to his moral behavior.

Discover what part David played in God's redemptive work in history.—Although he was capable of lofty friendship and heroic leadership, David was a sinful man. Yet God was at work in and through this vigorous ruler. God was sustaining his people, keeping alive hope in their hearts, leading them toward the fulfilment of his promise which finally came in Jesus Christ. Whatever appraisal is made of the constructive and destructive forces in David's life, he was a link, not a perfect link but a strong link, in the history of the people of God.[1]

The procedures outlined for a study of the life of David can be used in the quest for a deeper knowledge of any of the persons portrayed in the Bible. In each instance five questions are appropriate: (1) *Who was this person and what information about him is available in the Bible?* (2) *What crucial decisions were made by him as an individual or by a group of which he was a member?* (3) *What were the causes with which he was identified and the tasks to which he devoted his intelligence and energy?* (4) *What were the distinctive qualities of his character?* (5) *What part did he play in the history of the people of God?*

Study the Central Themes of the Bible

One of the values of a thoughtful reading of the Bible as a whole is the discovery of the central and unifying themes of the biblical message. These themes can be traced through the Old and New Testaments and are helpful in the quest for a coherent interpretation of life.

So that you will be alert to the major themes of the biblical message, list in your notebook three or four of the central themes of each book of the Bible as you read it. After you have completed the rapid reading of the books of the Bible, make a list of all the different themes you have recorded. Then select five or six of those which

[1] John Bright, *The Authority of the Old Testament* (New York: Abingdon Press, 1967), pp. 226–33.

occur most frequently in your list. In this way you will discover for yourself a few of the central themes of the biblical message. At a later date you may decide to trace one or more of these themes through the major divisions of the Old Testament and of the New Testament.

You may wish to compare your list of central themes with the following list:

The living God knows man as he is and loves him. This love is expressed in God's redemptive acts in the history of his people.

The supreme manifestation of God's redemptive purpose is his decisive action in the ministry, death, and resurrection of Jesus Christ. The Old Testament looks forward to the fulfilment of God's promise to his people in this decisive action. The New Testament interprets all events in the light of this decisive action.

The people of God at their best respond affirmatively to his redemptive action, commit themselves without selfish reservation to him, worship him, rely upon him, and obey his will.

Obedience to God's will includes compassion for companions on the human pilgrimage. This means accepting the neighbor, loving the neighbor, speaking truth to the neighbor, seeking justice for the neighbor, proclaiming the gospel to the neighbor, teaching the neighbor the Christian way of life.

Every dimension of man's life has been hurt by sin, and the remedy for sin is forgiveness. Forgiveness means setting a thing right insofar as it can be set right and includes justice and love. Love is an attitude of goodwill. It comes from God to man through Christ, fulfils the law, is a cohesive force in the community of faith, and produces courage to overcome evil with good.

(For more ideas on themes of the Bible and how to discover them, see pp. 108–112 in this book.)

Study the Books of the Bible

This is one of the most effective methods of Bible study. After you have exposed your mind to the total message of the Bible by reading it rapidly, make a thorough study of the books of the Bible which impressed you as vital parts of the biblical message directly related to your life at this time.

A few clues to an effective study of a book of the Bible deserve consideration:

Read the book of the Bible before you read commentaries on the book.—This will give you firsthand knowledge of the substance of the book itself, including the subjects discussed and the language used by the author.

Read the entire book.—A fundamental principle of research is to use the primary source (the Bible itself) and to examine the book as a whole. A second principle of research is to interpret the data honestly. These principles are employed in a serious study of the structure of thought, the key words, the dynamic personalities, and the central themes of a book of the Bible.

Study the book closely, using the best available tools of biblical scholarship.—Make your own outline of the message of the book. This will enable you to see clearly the writer's purpose, the type of literature he used, the specific subjects he included, the characters he introduced, the events he recorded, the places where the events took place, and, in some instances, the author's appraisal of the events. Use a Bible atlas to locate on a map each place mentioned in the book. Use a Bible dictionary or commentary to learn the meaning of the terms used. Who were the people to whom the book was addressed? What do you think they heard the author saying to them? The book is addressed to us also. What do we hear the author saying to us? If the author identified himself in the book, use a Bible dictionary and one or more commentaries to learn who he was and what the scholars say about him.

A thorough study of the Bible, a book at a time, stimulates our minds, sharpens our theological insights, strengthens our confidence in the power of truth, enlarges our knowledge of God, prepares us for worship, and improves our professional competence. John A. Broadus became a productive scholar and an effective teacher, one of the most highly respected men in American theological education. As a student at the University of Virginia, he was influenced profoundly by a paragraph written by John Locke concerning the importance of reading the Bible a book at a time.[2] This practice provided Broadus with an excellent beginning as a Bible student.

One approach to the message of 2 Corinthians will show how a book of the Bible may be studied in English. What is suggested here could be used as a guide in other studies of Bible material.

This writer was invited to teach a large Bible study group at Ridgecrest Baptist Assembly in the summer of 1967. Second Corinthians was the book chosen to be studied, based on the outline that follows. Each member of the group was encouraged to use whatever translation of the book he preferred.

---

[2] John A. Broadus, *Sermons and Addresses* (Baltimore: H. M. Wharton and Co., 1886), p. 171.

A Message from a Christian Thinker:
2 Corinthians

I. Preliminary considerations

    1. This study of 2 Corinthians is based upon the English text, but reference will be made to exegetical as well as expository commentaries written by competent and devout scholars. "A Critical and Exegetical Commentary on the Second Epistle of St. Paul to the Corinthians" by Alfred Plummer, published by Charles Scribner's Sons in 1915, remains the best commentary on 2 Corinthians in English. The exegesis of 2 Corinthians by Floyd Filson and the exposition of the epistle by James Reid in Volume 10 of the "Interpreter's Bible" are also useful.

    2. Paul was a Christian thinker and an effective missionary. He had Hebrew ancestry, Roman citizenship, and Greek culture. He interpreted life in the perspective of God's redemptive purpose, the relation of Christ to the Father, and the work of the Holy Spirit.

    3. The structure of this letter presents complex problems. There are able and reverent biblical scholars who think that the letter in its present form is a combination of letters by Paul to the Christian church in the dynamic city of Corinth. They argue that chapters 10–13 of 2 Corinthians are a part of the severe letter to which Paul refers in 2 Corinthians 2:3–4. The entire text of 2 Corinthians is found in the ancient and excellent manuscripts, Codex Vaticanus and Codex Sinaiticus. We do not know how much time may have elapsed between the writing of chapters 1–9 and chapters 10–13 of this letter. Furthermore, the letter has been transmitted as a whole and there is no question about its authenticity. The style, vocabulary, and thought are in harmony with the writings of Paul.

    4. The city of Corinth was burned in 146 B.C. and refounded as a Roman colony in 44 B.C.[3] In Paul's day the city had recovered its commercial prosperity, attracted immigrants from the whole Mediterranean world, and had a reputation as a city of pleasure. The tendency to disregard moral standards and to discount the value of fellowship was reflected in the Christian church established there and made it difficult for Paul to maintain the unity of the young church.[4]

II. Central themes in the message of 2 Corinthians

    The statement in the salutation concerning saints in "all Achaia" indicates an outreach of the Christian gospel from the city of Corinth.[5]

    1. The assurance that God comforts the true believer in every affliction (1:3–11)

    We belong to the creation as well as to the Creator, and we are exposed to peril and pain.

---

[3] *The Interpreter's Dictionary of the Bible* (New York: Abingdon Press, 1962), I, 682.

[4] Ernest Findlay Scott, *The Literature of the New Testament* (New York: Columbia University Press, 1932), p. 128.

[5] *The Westminster Historical Atlas to the Bible*, ed. George Ernest Wright and Floyd Vivian Filson (Philadelphia: The Westminster Press, 1945), p. 102.

We have no completely adequate rationale of human suffering, but we know that God is with us in every moment of every affliction.

God comforts his people in each affliction and enlarges their capacity to comfort others when they are in trouble. In five verses (1:3–7) Paul used the word "comfort," noun or verb, ten times. Comfort means companionship, encouragement, possession of inner resources to endure the strain of any difficulty on the human pilgrimage. We pray for those for whom we care; they pray for us; and this ministry of prayer is a source of comfort.

2. The Christian ministry interpreted by Paul (1:12 to 7:16)

Paul was writing about his ministry, but he had in mind also the ministry of Jesus and the ministry of the people of God who are committed to Jesus Christ.

Paul mentioned five characteristics of a good minister of Jesus Christ: (1) He has a sense of mission, of appointment, of high purpose (1:21). (2) He is competent for the task to which he is committed (3:5). The word translated "sufficiency" means "fitness" and "competence." (3) He maintains personal integrity (4:2). He refuses to practice the cunning spirit of this world and speaks the truth in friendly candor. (4) He participates in the ministry of reconciliation (5:17–20). (5) He does not lose heart (4:16). He has faith in God and confidence in the people with whom he works (7:16).

3. The Christian concern for the well-being of persons expressed in the sharing of material resources (8:1 to 9:15)

Paul invited the Christians of Corinth to participate in the offering for the saints in Jerusalem, and he asked and expected generosity in order to help meet the needs of persons in distress.

Participation in Christian giving to causes which deserve support emerges out of personal commitment to Jesus Christ (8:5). It is voluntary and generous (9:7–8). A Christian asks not how little but how much he can give. This kind of giving strengthens the bond of Christian fellowship and creates an attitude of gratitude to God for his inexpressible gift (9:13–15).

4. The response of a Christian thinker to the criticism of opponents in a church (10:1 to 13:14)

In reply to an attack on his personal character and apostolic authority by a group of critics which threatened to fracture the fellowship of the Christian church at Corinth, Paul refuted the charges with clarity and conviction.

In dealing with criticism Paul thought first of the reasonableness and graciousness of Jesus Christ. He wrote of the gentleness, the fairness, the considerateness of the Master. The word "considerateness" means (1) the refusal to press one's claim to the extreme, and (2) the readiness to consider and to prefer the well-being of another person.

Paul understood that criticism of a person is a sharp instrument and is to be used with utmost care. He replied to the unfair criticism directed at him on a very high level of objectivity. His critics had said that he was insincere and fickle. He answered that he had been honest and forthright and that "as surely as God is

faithful," his Yes has meant Yes and his No has meant No. His
critics had said that he was not an effective speaker. He replied
that, whatever appraisal had been made of him as a speaker, he
was not deficient in knowledge. His opponents had accused him of
seeking financial advantage for himself. He replied that other
churches had supported him while he served in the city of Corinth.

After answering the specific charges made against him, Paul
identified his opponents as "false apostles, deceitful workmen, dis-
guising themselves as apostles of Christ" (11:13, RSV); and, although he was willing to endure "insults, hardships, persecutions"
at their hands (12:10), he was unwilling for them to distort the truth
about Jesus Christ, to break the fellowship of the believers, and
to stir up "jealousy, anger, selfishness, slander, gossip, conceit, and
disorder" (12:20, RSV).

Paul prayed for his enemies as well as for his friends. The
benediction (13:14) is a prayer and includes all who might read it
or hear it read: "The grace of the Lord Jesus Christ and the love of
God and the fellowship of the Holy Spirit be with you all" (RSV).

This study of 2 Corinthians in English by a group of thoughtful
young people and adults involved three of the guidelines set forth in
this chapter. It was a serious and sincere study of an entire book of
the Bible with attention to the precise meaning of key words and
central themes. The relevance of the message to the problem of
human suffering, the characteristics of Christian ministry, the sharing
of resources to meet human need, and a Christian approach to
bitterly unjust criticisms was clearly evident. All the tools of biblical
study recommended in chapter 2 were employed, including many
different translations of the Bible.

There are thousands of thoughtful people in our churches who
read more than one hundred pages per week of contemporary literature. Such reading is important, for it enriches the quality of life in
the homes, in the community, in the church, and in the nation. This
type of reading should be continued. But there needs to be added
specific time and attention to the serious study of the Word of God.
The series of books, of which this is the second, has been designed to
be used in such a study. Volumes 3 through 8 will take the student
through a survey of the entire Bible. Annual Bible Study books,
released for use each January, will provide opportunities for more
thorough study of books of the Bible. *The Broadman Bible Commentary,* which is now available, will provide enriching reading for serious
Bible students.

**Enrichment Resources
for Chapter 4**

Guidelines for Effective Bible Study

Through the Bible in Thirteen Weeks
Notebook of Bible Readings (Sample)
Central Themes of the Bible—*Morris Ashcraft*
Key Words of the Bible—*D. P. Brooks*
My Bible Reading Record (chart, American Bible Society)

Through the Bible in Thirteen Weeks

Plan suggested by Olin T. Binkley

DATE BEGUN

Week 1 *

Sun.—Mark 1–10 ☐
Mon.—Mark 11–16; Matthew 1–4 ☐
Tues.—Matthew 5–15 ☐
Wed.—Matthew 16–26 ☐
Thurs.—Matthew 27 to Luke 6 ☐
Fri.—Luke 7–15 ☐
Sat.—Luke 16–24 ☐

Week 2

Sun.—John 1–10 ☐
Mon.—John 11–21 ☐
Tues.—Genesis 1–16 ☐
Wed.—Genesis 17–28 ☐
Thurs.—Genesis 29–40 ☐
Fri.—Genesis 41 to Exodus 2 ☐
Sat.—Exodus 3–14 ☐

Week 3

Sun.—Exodus 15–27 ☐
Mon.—Exodus 28–40 ☐
Tues.—Leviticus 1–13 ☐
Wed.—Leviticus 14–24 ☐
Thurs.—Leviticus 25 to Numbers 5 ☐
Fri.—Numbers 6–15 ☐
Sat.—Numbers 16–26 ☐

Week 4

Sun.—Numbers 27 to Deuteronomy 2 ☐
Mon.—Deuteronomy 3–13 ☐
Tues.—Deuteronomy 14–27 ☐
Wed.—Deuteronomy 28 to Joshua 3 ☐
Thurs.—Joshua 4–14 ☐
Fri.—Joshua 15 to Judges 2 ☐
Sat.—Judges 3–12 ☐

Week 5

Sun.—Judges 13–21 ☐
Mon.—1 Samuel 1–14 ☐
Tues.—1 Samuel 15–25 ☐
Wed.—1 Samuel 26 to 2 Samuel 8 ☐
Thurs.—2 Samuel 9–19 ☐
Fri.—2 Samuel 20 to 1 Kings 4 ☐
Sat.—1 Kings 5–12 ☐

Week 6

Sun.—1 Kings 13–22 ☐
Mon.—2 Kings 1–10 ☐
Tues.—2 Kings 11–25 ☐
Wed.—Isaiah 1–12 ☐
Thurs.—Isaiah 13–26 ☐
Fri.—Isaiah 27–38 ☐
Sat.—Isaiah 39–48 ☐

Week 7

Sun.—Isaiah 49–60 ☐
Mon.—Isaiah 61 to Jeremiah 3 ☐
Tues.—Jeremiah 4–13 ☐
Wed.—Jeremiah 14–25 ☐
Thurs.—Jeremiah 26–36 ☐
Fri.—Jeremiah 37–47 ☐
Sat.—Jeremiah 48–52 ☐

Week 8

Sun.—Ezekiel 1–14 ☐
Mon.—Ezekiel 15–23 ☐
Tues.—Ezekiel 24–34 ☐
Wed.—Ezekiel 35–45 ☐
Thurs.—Ezekiel 46–48; Hosea 1 to
Joel 3 ☐
Fri.—Amos 1 to Micah 7 ☐
Sat.—Nahum 1 to Zephaniah 3 ☐

Week 9

Sun.—Haggai 1 to Malachi 4 ☐
Mon.—Psalms 1–26 ☐
Tues.—Psalms 27–51 ☐
Wed.—Psalms 52–77 ☐
Thurs.—Psalms 78–98 ☐
Fri.—Psalms 99–117 ☐
Sat.—Psalms 118–142 ☐

Week 10

Sun.—Psalms 143 to Proverbs 11 ☐
Mon.—Proverbs 12–25 ☐
Tues.—Proverbs 26–31; Job 1–9 ☐
Wed.—Job 10–27 ☐
Thurs.—Job 28–42 ☐
Fri.—Ruth; Solomon; Lamentations ☐
Sat.—Ecclesiastes; Esther 1–4 ☐

Week 11

Sun.—Esther 5–10; Daniel 1–7 ☐
Mon.—Daniel 8–12; Ezra ☐
Tues.—Nehemiah ☐
Wed.—1 Chronicles 1–7 ☐
Thurs.—1 Chronicles 8–21 ☐
Fri.—1 Chronicles 22 to 2 Chronicles 6 ☐
Sat.—2 Chronicles 7–22 ☐

Week 12

Sun.—2 Chronicles 23–36 ☐
Mon.—Acts 1–12 ☐
Tues.—Acts 13–24 ☐
Wed.—Acts 25 to Romans 7 ☐
Thurs.—Romans 8 to 1 Corinthians 7 ☐
Fri.—1 Corinthians 8 to 2 Corinthians 9 ☐
Sat.—2 Corinthians 10 to Ephesians 6 ☐

Week 13

Sun.—Philippians 1 to 2 Thessalonians 3 ☐
Mon.—1 Timothy 1 to Hebrews 6 ☐
Tues.—Hebrews 7 to 1 Peter 2 ☐
Wed.—1 Peter 3 to 3 John ☐
Thurs.—Jude to Revelation 12 ☐
Fri.—Revelation 13–22 ☐

DATE COMPLETED

* Check each day's assignment as read.

Notebook of Bible Readings (Sample)
Week 1, Friday

1. **Reference:** Luke 7–15

2. **Some key words:** authority; faith; demons; forgiveness

3. **Outstanding personalities:** centurion; widow of Nain; John the Baptist; Mary Magdalene; Simon; the demoniac; Jairus; Herod; boy with loaves and fish; Peter, James, and John; Mary; Martha

4. **Central themes:** Jesus' ministry outside the synagogue; Jesus' concern for all people; Jesus' true followers shown to be those who hear and do God's will; exposing of Pharisees

(NOTE: I would like to come back and study more carefully the teachings of all these parables.)

5. **Quotations** (I may memorize some of these):

> Then Jesus answering said unto them, Go your way, and tell John what things ye have seen and heard; how that the blind see, the lame walk, the lepers are cleansed, the deaf hear, the dead are raised, to the poor the gospel is preached (7:22).

> Wherefore I say unto thee, Her sins, which are many, are forgiven; for she loved much: but to whom little is forgiven, the same loveth little (7:47).

> And he said to them all, If any man will come after me, let him deny himself, and take up his cross daily, and follow me (9:23).

> Therefore said he unto them, The harvest truly is great, but the labourers are few: pray ye therefore the Lord of the harvest, that he would send forth labourers into his harvest (10:2).

> Consider the lilies how they grow: they toil not, they spin not; and yet I say unto you, that Solomon in all his glory was not arrayed like one of these. If then God so clothe the grass, which is to-day in the field, and to-morrow is cast into the oven; how much more will he clothe you, O ye of little faith? (12:27–28).

> But rather seek ye the kingdom of God; and all these things shall be added unto you (12:31).

6. **Questions for further study:** What is today's lesson from the parable of the sower? What does 8:17 mean? Were those real demons in the Gadarene demoniac? What did Jesus mean in 9:27? What is the significance of "he set his face to go to Jerusalem" in 9:51? Did Peter know the significance of what he was saying on the mount of transfiguration?

Central Themes of the Bible
Morris Ashcraft

One method of Bible study has been suggested in which the student looks for the great central themes of the Bible. Dr. Binkley identified these themes by noting them in his reading and then by choosing those which appeared most frequently. (See p. 99.) In this article, three ways are suggested for studying the Bible by central themes. These three methods are distinguished from each other only in the manner in which the themes are chosen and the choice of sources employed in their study.

Begin with a statement of the central themes of the Bible as they have been given by some competent scholar in the field. These will usually appear as central themes of the Old and New Testaments. This method is highly recommended because rarely does a beginning Bible student possess the discernment to recognize these themes simply by reading the Bible.

Norman H. Snaith in *The Distinctive Ideas of the Old Testament* lists these ideas as: (1) the holiness of God; (2) the righteousness of God; (3) the salvation of God; (4) the covenant-love of God; (5) the election-love of God; and (6) the Spirit of God. Obviously, there are many more great themes in the Old Testament than these "distinctive" ones.

A more comprehensive statement of such themes can be found in the introductory articles in commentaries. A good example is G. Ernest Wright's article, "The Faith of Israel," in volume 1 of *The Interpreter's Bible*. A student should select some good source which briefly outlines the faith of Israel in the Old Testament and the Christian faith in the New Testament and thereby discern the central themes of the two Testaments. Then he should study the Bible by tracing these themes using a concordance, Bible dictionary, and commentary.

H. Wheeler Robinson in *The Religious Ideas of the Old Testament* lists the major ideas as: (1) the idea of religion; (2) the idea of God; (3) the idea of man; (4) the approach of God to man; (5) the approach of man to God; (6) the problem of sin and suffering; and (7) the hope of the nation.

Dr. Ashcraft is professor of theology, Midwestern Baptist Theological Seminary, Kansas City, Missouri.

Another source of help in selecting these themes for study is doctrinal or theological literature. Every theology of the Old Testament or of the New Testament will outline the central themes as understood by the author of the particular book. Every book of Christian doctrine attempts to state these themes and suggests the scriptural foundation for them. Most denominations have creedal statements or confessions of faith in which they list the major themes of biblical faith as they understand them. These statements usually have biblical references which will be useful as guidelines in study.

Another way of getting at the major themes of the Bible is to seek answers to the major questions arising from man's religious life. With these questions in mind, one studies the Bible for the answers. A number of these questions stand out: (1) What is God really like? (2) What is the nature of man? (3) What is sin? (4) Why is man so prone to turn against God? (5) What does God expect of man? (6) How does God forgive sin? (7) How can man know God? (8) Did Jesus Christ really show us God? (9) What can man expect beyond this life?

In all of these variations, the Bible student must find the biblical information on the specific subjects. He can do this by following suggestions in the sources cited, by checking the key words involved, and by noting them as he reads carefully.

In the Old Testament, these ideas include God in his own nature and in relationship to the world which he has made. He is Creator of the world and of man. God created man in his own image, but man through sin turned away from God. God loved man enough to seek his salvation, and he did this through the covenant relation with Israel. God sent the prophets to proclaim his word of repentance toward God and justice toward man.

In the New Testament, one finds the same emphases along with a fuller disclosure of God. The kingdom of God has come in Jesus Christ. Jesus was the fulfilment of Old Testament hopes. He was the Son of God and Saviour of the world. Jesus died and was raised to secure forgiveness of man's sins. To have faith in Christ is to be saved, born again, created anew. The man believing in Christ is transformed into the image of God. The followers of Jesus must love other men as Christ has loved them. Christians must share their good news with others. Because Christ was raised from the dead, his followers live in hope of eternal life.

Another method for identifying the central themes of the Bible is to identify and study the key words of the Bible. We have given emphasis to word study, but we consider it now as a way to discover central themes. The identification is not difficult. Even the casual listener or reader of the Bible can recognize the more common terms in biblical faith, such as God, man, sin, salvation, justification, grace, repentance, faith, forgiveness, love, hope, judgment, reconciliation, resurrection, and heaven. Books of theology and doctrine will usually list these most significant terms. There are volumes published for this particular purpose such as the one by Alan Richardson, *A Theological Word Book of the Bible* (chap. 2, p. 23).

Having determined some of the more important terms in the Bible, one begins the study by referring to a concordance to locate the passages for study. Or, one may refer to a Bible dictionary which will give not only the Scripture references but an outline of study and some very helpful guidance. Reference has already been made to the use of Bible dictionaries. Let us assume that we are interested in the biblical term "image of God" as we try to understand the nature of man. We turn in *The Interpreter's Dictionary of the Bible* to the article "Image of God." (It is found in Vol. II, pp. 682–85.) All biblical passages are listed and discussed. Other passages which do not mention the "image of God" but seem to allude to it are discussed. The Old Testament idea is discussed in relation to the development of the idea found in the New Testament. This article gives a very thorough understanding of this great theme in biblical thought.

There are two advantages in studying the great themes of the Bible by identifying the important terms: The study can be carried on with a minimum of tools and can be expanded into a very thorough use of other sources. The study can begin on an elementary level with a limited number of terms and can be expanded into a comprehensive and detailed study on a very advanced level.

A third approach to the study of the Bible through the study of central themes is to select the main theme of each biblical book as the starting point. This plan has several advantages. Each book is different, and studying in this manner is much more in keeping with sound principles of biblical study. Approaching Bible study on the individual biblical book basis would improve the two plans previously suggested. Furthermore, if one can state the central theme of a biblical book succinctly, he will be able to remember the book and its teaching. The topical study previously outlined leaves much to be desired from the standpoint of memory.

There are disadvantages in this method. It is not always easy or possible to discern this central theme. Some books are quite difficult when one tries to isolate the theme. Another disadvantage is that one must usually depend upon some source for help in determining the central theme. But this is the problem in all Bible study. Every student must accept guidance from some teacher as he begins his study. He must look at the introductory material in a commentary on the book he is studying. In that discussion he will find the "purpose" of the author or theme of the writing. He must know this as he reads the book unless he has unusual discernment or previous experience.

Some writers of biblical books state rather clearly the themes of their compositions. For instance, Micah tried to call Judah to return to God. His whole message is summarized in the words, "He has showed you, O man, what is good; and what does the Lord require of you but to do justice, and to love kindness, and to walk humbly with your God?" (6:8, RSV). Amos condemned Israel for her rejection of God. She was religious in official ceremony but godless in all of her ways. Amos saw God's judgment coming on the nation because of this sin. The greatest evidence of Israel's godlessness was her oppression of and injustice to people. He cried out, "But let justice roll down like waters, and righteousness like an everflowing stream" (5:24, RSV). Likewise, the author of the Fourth Gospel stated his purpose in the whole gospel when he said, "Now Jesus did many other signs in the presence of the disciples, which are not written in this book; but these are written that you may believe that Jesus is the Christ, the Son of God, and that believing you may have life in his name" (John 20:30-31, RSV).

Some biblical books develop a single large theme even though it may not be stated in a single sentence within the book. Many New Testament scholars agree that the dominant theme of both Romans and Galatians is that "justification is by faith in Jesus Christ and not by keeping the ceremonial law." Knowing this does not guarantee one that he will understand all of both books, but it surely gives him important guidance.

It is more difficult to state the theme of a book like Acts, which includes so much history. There is a heavy emphasis upon the work of the Holy Spirit. The first part of the book deals more with the leadership of Peter and the latter part with that of Paul. The story begins with the small band of disciples awaiting the coming of the Lord and ends with Paul in jail at Rome. What is the theme of the book of Acts? Is it the fact that the Holy Spirit led the Christians from their Jewish beginning to a universal faith? Is it the story of the expansion of Christianity from Jerusalem to Rome, from Jew to Gentile breaking down all the barriers to the gospel? It would seem that to know this theme is to give considerable help in reading the book and in relating it to the rest of the Bible.

Each one of these methods will help one study the Bible. Each leads to a fuller view of the great ideas in the Bible, and in time will lead one into a coherent view of God and man and his relationship to God. The constant reevaluation and rearrangement of the elements of faith form the necessary human struggle in working out one's own understanding of his own salvation.

Key Words of the Bible
D. P. Brooks

Words are the basic symbols of communication. The message of the Bible comes to us in written words. Biblical writers had clear pictures in their minds when they penned the words of the Scriptures. We need to attempt to get the right pictures by understanding words. Only those who understand Hebrew and Greek can read the original words spoken or recorded by the biblical writers. Those who read in an English translation need to remember that they are reading English words that are not a perfect match for the words in the original, even though we have good English translations. For many of the key words of the Bible there is no English equivalent. Thus, every student of the Bible must go behind the English word and try to discover the meaning of the original Hebrew or Greek word it attempts to represent. It is especially important that the key words of the Bible be allowed to say to us what they said to those who first read the biblical passage.

If we had to pick *the* key word of the Old Testament, it probably would be the word "covenant." The covenant was the core of Israel's faith, with all other aspects of their religion clustering around this concept. This concept is so significant in both parts of our Bible that we properly call the two parts Old Covenant (Testament) and New Covenant (Testament). What is the meaning of this word which is used over 250 times in the Old Testament alone?

The Hebrew word *berith* (covenant) probably goes back to a root word meaning bond or fetter. To make, or cut, a covenant was to forge bonds between two parties, binding them into a solemn agreement, a league. A covenant created a kind of brotherhood. Blood was prominent in sealing covenants (Gen. 15). Covenants were made in the ancient world between persons, as between Jonathan and David (1 Sam. 18:3–5). Judas made a covenant with the authorities to betray Jesus (Matt. 26:15). Marriage was a covenant between a man and his wife (Mal. 2:14). Covenants were common between tribes, between nations, and between a ruler and his people. The historian wrote: "Then all the tribes of Israel came to David at Hebron, and said, 'Behold, we are your bone and flesh. In times past, when Saul was king over us, it was you that led out and brought in Israel; and the Lord said to you, "You shall be shepherd of my people Israel, and you shall be prince over Israel.' " So all the elders of Israel came to the king at Hebron; and King David made a covenant with them at Hebron before the Lord, and they anointed David king over Israel" (2 Sam. 5:1–3, RSV).

There were two basic types of covenant: the parity and the suzerainty. When equals made an agreement, it was a parity covenant; when a greater granted a treaty to a lesser, it was a suzerainty covenant. For example, during most of the years of the divided kingdom, Judah was a vassal of one of the great powers. Assyria first and then Babylon forced Judah to make an alliance that reduced the small nation into a position of subservience to the superpower. Jeremiah declared that Judah must honor her covenant with Babylon or suffer destruction because it was God's punishment on the nation for breaking her covenant with God. A powerful nation could destroy a small enemy nation, or it could grant the small nation a covenant. The covenant spelled out the duties of the inferior while offering the protection of the superior power.

Obviously, Israel's covenant with God was of the suzerainty type. God first delivered Israel from bondage, thus putting them in debt to him. Then, out of his goodness, God offered Israel a covenant. If Israel would be true to God and live under his authority and law, he would be her Saviour-God. The giving of the law was a part of the covenant and spelled out the kind of life and covenant demanded of Israel. Severe penalties were provided in case Israel broke the covenant.

No one can make sense of the Old Testament apart from the covenant concept. Each time a prophet called on the people to repent and return to God it was a call to renew the covenant and live by its demands. Furthermore, Israel came into being as a nation because of the covenant; and she disintegrated and became easy prey to foreign powers when she forsook her covenant and became "like the nations." Her history is the story of violations of the covenant and of covenant renewal.

The covenant concept passes over into the New Testament, with the new people of God, the church, becoming the "new Israel," the chosen people. Jeremiah had prophesied the establishment of a new covenant that would be cut in the hearts of men rather than in stone tablets. Jesus interpreted his death as the establishing of the new covenant: " 'This cup is the new covenant in my blood' " (1 Cor. 11:25, RSV).

For descriptions of ancient covenants, read Genesis 15 and Exodus 24. For a record of a covenant renewal ceremony, see Joshua 23–24.

For an idea of the way "covenant" is used in the New Testament, check these references: Luke 1:72; Galatians 3:17; Hebrews 7:22; 8:9–13; 9:20; Acts 7:8; 2 Corinthians 3:14; Mark 14:24. It is used as a verb and sometimes translated "agreed" in John 9:22; Acts 23:20; "to assent" in Acts 24:9; and "to covenant" in Luke 22:5. Read these verses and see a commentary on them for a better understanding of the covenant idea in the New Testament.

Another of the key words of the Bible is the word "love." There are at least six Hebrew words that can be translated love. *Aheb* refers primarily to passionate love between man and woman, but is also used to express family affection and friendship. This word occurs over two hundred times in the Old Testament. *Chasaq* has about the same meaning as *aheb*. *Chaphets* refers to delight in someone or something, and *ratsah* means to accept or be pleased. *Chanan* refers to the condescension of the rich to the poor. But the richest of all Hebrew words for love is *hesed,* which expresses loyalty and the conduct that befits loyalty. This word is translated "lovingkindness" in the King James Version and "steadfast love" in the Revised Standard Version. It is because of the power of God's *hesed* (loyal love) that he does not destroy the people when they break the covenant. Steadfast love is the key concept in picturing God's character and indicating his attitude toward his erring people. And the people of God are expected to return his love by being loyal to the covenant, faithful in keeping the law.

There are several Greek words for love. *Eros* is sexual love, the love of a man for a woman. It refers to a love called forth by the worth or attractiveness of the one loved. Such love seeks to possess the one who is loved. This word most closely parallels the common idea of love in our culture. How significant that this word does not occur in the New Testament!

Philia is social love, the affection of a man for his friend.

Storge expresses family affection.

Philadelphia expresses love between brothers and sisters.

Philanthropia is humanity, kindness, courtesy.

Agapē is the word most prominently used in the Greek New Testament. It refers to a love based in the will rather than in the emotions. *Agapē* love is God's kind of love, rooted in his own goodness rather than in any merit or worth of the one loved. The supreme expression of God's love is his sending Christ to die for us. Christians are to become like God in loving all men with unfailing goodwill. "God is love." Therefore, we are commanded to love even our enemies; and we are to love our Christian brothers as Jesus has loved us. All of this would be lost on the person who read the word "love" and saw no more than the Hollywood concept of romantic love, which the Greeks expressed by the word *eros*.

The word "soul" is one of the prominent biblical words which means something quite different in current English from the word the biblical writers used. According to Young's *Analytical Concordance of the Bible,* this word occurs in the King James Version of the Old Testament approximately 440 times. This word "soul," with two exceptions, translates the Hebrew word *nephesh,* which seems to go back to the idea of breath. A *nephesh* is a living being. For example, when we read that God breathed into man's nostrils the breath of life and he became a living soul, we must understand what the writer meant to say.

Perhaps the most commonplace concept of soul in our culture is that it refers to "that eternal part of man that survives death." Taking his cue from Greek philosophy, modern man tends to think of the soul as something that can exist apart from the body. Such an idea is entirely alien to Hebrew thought. Man does not have a soul; he *is* a soul. Throughout the Old Testament, the word "soul" stands for the entire person, body and spirit. Indeed, the soul is the union of body and spirit. Thus, when the writer says that man "became a living soul," he is saying that he became a living person. Modern translations help to clarify this meaning. Nowhere in the Old Testament do we find the idea of soul as something independent from the body.

In the New Testament, the Greek work *pseuche* translates the Hebrew *nephesh*. While there seems to be a development from the Old Testament idea, the typical thinking of the New Testament is in line with the Old. When the rich farmer said to himself: "Soul, . . . take thine ease" (Luke 12:19), he was not talking about an immortal essence that would survive death. He was talking to himself, using "soul" for "self." And when God said, "This night shall thy soul be required of thee," he was announcing the man's death. Similarly, when Jesus asked, "What is a man profited, if he shall gain the whole world, and lose his own soul? or what shall a man give in exchange for his soul?" (Matt. 16:26) he used the word *pseuche,* self. Therefore, the Revised Standard Version translates the verse as follows: " 'What will it profit a man, if he gains the whole world and forfeits his life? Or what shall a man give in return for his life?' " This does not lessen the peril indicated by Jesus' words. It heightens it. For to lose one's soul (life) is to lose everything.

There are English words that translate Hebrew or Greek words without any serious loss of meaning. But the key words of the Bible are so important that the serious student will insist on trying to get the exact picture that a word had for the original writer of the biblical book he is reading. And the more prominent a word is in the Bible, the more essential it is that we grasp its meaning accurately.

Without making any attempt to be exhaustive, here are some other key Bible words that, with all the meaning they have for us, still do not carry quite the depth of meaning as the original words they seek to translate: salvation, sin, hell, Rock, know, law, everlasting, redemption, fellowship, mystery, faith, repentance, perish, perfect, righteousness. This is only a beginning list. Each student will want to make his own list of key words of the Bible and then try to determine which ones call for further study. What could be more important to the Bible student than to improve his understanding of the key words that carry the message of God to man?

MY BIBLE READING RECORD

EXPLANATION OF CHART (on pp. 118–20):
Favorite chapters are indicated by bold face type. The various divisions indicate the unique arrangement of the canon of Scripture. In the New Testament (back page) it is suggested that the Gospel of Mark be read first, followed by the other Gospels. Next should come a study of the New Testament Book of History, The Acts, followed by the Pauline and General Epistles, and lastly the book of Revelation. (Check each chapter as it is read.)

You can read the entire Bible in a year by reading 15 minutes each day. A suggested breakdown would be three chapters every weekday and five on Sunday. But HOW you read is more important than how much you read.

1. Read alertly. Picture to yourself the situation.

2. Ask yourself the meaning of what you read; what it teaches you to BELIEVE, to BECOME, to DO.

3. Underline passages that can be personally helpful. Copy and memorize them. Discuss them with family or friends.

4. Keep a definite time for daily reading. Make it a habit, but always make it meaningful.

THE OLD TESTAMENT

Law   Starting date

Genesis	1	2	3	4	5	6	7	8	9	10	11	12	13	14	15	16
	17	18	19	20	21	22	23	24	25	26	27	28	29	30	31	32
	33	34	35	36	37	38	39	40	41	42	43	44	45	46	47	48
	49	50														
Exodus	1	2	3	4	5	6	7	8	9	10	11	12	13	14	15	16
	17	18	19	20	21	22	23	24	25	26	27	28	29	30	31	32
	33	34	35	36	37	38	39	40								
Leviticus	1	2	3	4	5	6	7	8	9	10	11	12	13	14	15	16
	17	18	19	20	21	22	23	24	25	26	27					
Numbers	1	2	3	4	5	6	7	8	9	10	11	12	13	14	15	16
	17	18	19	20	21	22	23	24	25	26	27	28	29	30	31	32
	33	34	35	36												
Deuteronomy	1	2	3	4	5	6	7	8	9	10	11	12	13	14	15	16
	17	18	19	20	21	22	23	24	25	26	27	28	29	30	31	32
	33	34														

History

Joshua	1	2	3	4	5	6	7	8	9	10	11	12	13	14	15	16
	17	18	19	20	21	22	23	24								
Judges	1	2	3	4	5	6	7	8	9	10	11	12	13	14	15	16
	17	18	19	20	21											
Ruth	1	2	3	4												
1 Samuel	1	2	3	4	5	6	7	8	9	10	11	12	13	14	15	16
	17	18	19	20	21	22	23	24	25	26	27	28	29	30	31	
2 Samuel	1	2	3	4	5	6	7	8	9	10	11	12	13	14	15	16
	17	18	19	20	21	22	23	24								
1 Kings	1	2	3	4	5	6	7	8	9	10	11	12	13	14	15	16
	17	18	19	20	21	22										
2 Kings	1	2	3	4	5	6	7	8	9	10	11	12	13	14	15	16
	17	18	19	20	21	22	23	24	25							
1 Chronicles	1	2	3	4	5	6	7	8	9	10	11	12	13	14	15	16
	17	18	19	20	21	22	23	24	25	26	27	28	29			
2 Chronicles	1	2	3	4	5	6	7	8	9	10	11	12	13	14	15	16
	17	18	19	20	21	22	23	24	25	26	27	28	29	30	31	32
	33	34	35	36												
Ezra	1	2	3	4	5	6	7	8	9	10						
Nehemiah	1	2	3	4	5	6	7	8	9	10	11	12	13			
Esther	1	2	3	4	5	6	7	8	9	10						

Poetry

Job	1	2	3	4	5	6	7	8	9	10	11	12	13	14	15	16
	17	18	19	20	21	22	23	24	25	26	27	28	29	30	31	32
	33	34	35	36	37	38	39	40	41	42						

Psalms	1	2	3	4	5	6	7	8	9	10	11	12	13	14	15	16
	17	18	**19**	20	21	22	**23**	**24**	25	26	**27**	28	29	30	31	32
	33	34	35	36	**37**	38	39	40	41	**42**	43	44	45	**46**	47	48
	49	50	**51**	52	53	54	55	56	57	58	59	60	61	62	63	64
	65	66	**67**	68	69	70	71	72	73	74	75	76	77	78	79	**80**
	81	82	83	**84**	85	86	87	88	89	**90**	**91**	92	**93**	94	**95**	96
	97	98	99	**100**	101	102	**103**	104	105	106	107	108	109	110	111	112
	113	114	115	116	117	118	119	120	**121**	122	123	124	125	126	127	128
	129	130	131	132	133	134	135	136	137	138	**139**	140	141	142	143	144
	145	**146**	147	**148**	149	150										
Proverbs	1	**2**	**3**	**4**	5	6	7	8	9	10	11	12	13	14	15	16
	17	18	19	20	21	22	23	24	25	26	27	28	29	**30**	**31**	
Ecclesiastes	1	2	**3**	4	5	6	7	8	9	10	11	**12**				
Song/Solomon	1	**2**	3	4	5	6	7	**8**								

Major prophets

Isaiah	1	**2**	3	4	5	**6**	7	8	9	10	**11**	12	13	14	15	16
	17	18	19	20	21	22	23	24	25	26	27	28	29	30	31	32
	33	34	**35**	36	37	38	39	**40**	41	**42**	**43**	44	45	46	47	48
	49	50	51	**52**	**53**	54	**55**	56	57	58	59	**60**	**61**	62	63	64
	65	66														
Jeremiah	1	2	**3**	4	5	6	7	8	**9**	10	11	**12**	13	14	15	16
	17	18	19	20	21	22	23	24	25	26	27	28	29	30	**31**	32
	33	34	35	36	37	38	39	40	41	42	43	44	45	46	47	48
	49	50	51	52												
Lamentations	1	2	3	4	**5**											
Ezekiel	1	2	3	4	5	6	7	8	9	10	11	12	13	14	15	16
	17	18	19	20	21	22	23	24	25	26	27	28	29	30	31	32
	33	**34**	35	36	**37**	38	39	40	41	42	43	44	45	46	47	48
Daniel	1	2	3	4	5	6	7	8	9	10	11	12				

Minor prophets

Hosea	1	2	3	**4**	5	6	7	8	9	10	**11**	12	13	**14**	
Joel	1	2	3												
Amos	1	**2**	3	4	**5**	6	7	8	9						
Obadiah	1														
Jonah	1	2	3	4											
Micah	1	2	3	4	5	**6**	**7**								
Nahum	1	2	3												
Habakkuk	1	**2**	3												
Zephaniah	1	2	3												
Haggai	1	**2**													
Zechariah	1	2	3	4	5	6	7	**8**	9	10	11	12	13	14	
Malachi	1	2	**3**	**4**											

THE NEW TESTAMENT

Gospels

	1	2	3	4	5	6	7	8	9	10	11	12	13	14	15	16
Matthew	1	2	3	4	5	6	7	8	9	10	11	12	13	14	15	16
	17	18	19	20	21	22	23	24	25	26	27	28				
Mark	1	2	3	4	5	6	7	8	9	10	11	12	13	14	15	16
Luke	1	2	3	4	5	6	7	8	9	10	11	12	13	14	15	16
	17	18	19	20	21	22	23	24								
John	1	2	3	4	5	6	7	8	9	10	11	12	13	14	15	16
	17	18	19	20	21											

New Testament History

	1	2	3	4	5	6	7	8	9	10	11	12	13	14	15	16
Acts	1	2	3	4	5	6	7	8	9	10	11	12	13	14	15	16
	17	18	19	20	21	22	23	24	25	26	27	28				

Pauline Epistles

	1	2	3	4	5	6	7	8	9	10	11	12	13	14	15	16
Romans	1	2	3	4	5	6	7	8	9	10	11	12	13	14	15	16
1 Corinthians	1	2	3	4	5	6	7	8	9	10	11	12	13	14	15	16
2 Corinthians	1	2	3	4	5	6	7	8	9	10	11	12	13			
Galatians	1	2	3	4	5	6										
Ephesians	1	2	3	4	5	6										
Philippians	1	2	3	4												
Colossians	1	2	3	4												
1 Thess.	1	2	3	4	5											
2 Thess.	1	2	3													
1 Timothy	1	2	3	4	5	6										
2 Timothy	1	2	3	4												
Titus	1	2	3													
Philemon	1															
*Hebrews	1	2	3	4	5	6	7	8	9	10	11	12	13			

General Epistles

	1	2	3	4	5											
James	1	2	3	4	5											
1 Peter	1	2	3	4	5											
2 Peter	1	2	3													
1 John	1	2	3	4	5											
2 John	1															
3 John	1															
Jude	1															

New Testament Prophecy

	1	2	3	4	5	6	7	8	9	10	11	12	13	14	15	16
Revelation	1	2	3	4	5	6	7	8	9	10	11	12	13	14	15	16
	17	18	19	20	21	22										

* Authorship uncertain.

CHAPTER FIVE

Wise Decision
and
Right Action

This study has been developed as answers to five questions: (1) Why study the Bible today? What values are derived from a thorough study of the Bible? (2) What resources are available to Christian laymen for Bible study? (3) What principles of interpretation of the Bible are guides to a trustworthy understanding of its message? (4) What guidelines are helpful in the development of a sensible and useful plan of Bible study? (5) Is the message of the Bible relevant to wise decision and right action in daily living?

In preceding chapters we have examined the first four of these questions. It remains for us to explore the ways in which the message of the Bible equips our minds and hearts for wise decision and right action on the front line of conscience and compassion in the contemporary world.

In view of what God has said to us through his servants in the history of Israel and in response to what he has done for us in Jesus Christ, what should we say and do in the concrete situations in which we speak and act here and now? What should we say and do in the family, the church, and the community? The search for a reliable answer to this question is illuminated by interpreters in many areas of human thought and endeavor.

What are the most lucid and informed thinkers saying about cultural patterns, moral values, technological advances, and intergroup conflicts? Their interpretation of what is taking place in the world today merits attention. It is not, however, the whole story.

In addition to descriptive studies of the contexts of human life at this point in history, we have access to the primary documents of the Christian faith. We search the Scriptures for light on fundamental questions about God and man, personal identity and interpersonal competence, righteousness and love, sin and salvation, duty and destiny. We do not *make* the Bible relevant to the most urgent issues confronting us. It *is* relevant. How do we discover the ways by which the Bible corrects and refines our presuppositions and influences our decisions and actions? We draw attention to four vital factors.

The Bible Is Primarily a Book About God and His People.

Although we appreciate its historical data and the literary beauty of many of its passages, the central purpose of the Bible is to present a religious and moral message. In its pages we find a record of God's revelation of himself through what he has done for men and what he has said to men, and also an account of the ways men have responded to him affirmatively and negatively.

We discover, as we read the books of the Bible, that across the centuries God has revealed himself as Creator, Judge, and Redeemer. Accordingly, we study the Bible to get acquainted with the living God who is active in creation, judgment, and redemption and to learn how to respond appropriately to him.

The law set forth in the Old Testament is essentially a religious and moral message.—It is the articulation of God's will for his people. They are to accept it as instruction from him and to obey it with the assurance that he is the God of justice.

> **The Rock, his work is perfect;**
>   **for all his ways are justice.**
> **A God of faithfulness and without iniquity,**
>   **just and right is he.**
>   **—Deuteronomy 32:4, RSV**

The legal codes preserved in the Old Testament place high value upon the integrity of God, the sacredness of the family, and the worth of human life. These codes have a distinctively religious basis, and they are addressed to people who are responsible not primarily to human leaders but to God.

The prophets were creative leaders in the history and religion of Israel.—They had a strong sense of mission. They were convinced that God had spoken to them and that he was speaking through them. Their writings which have been preserved in the Old Testament are charged with profound religious insight. This religious insight is the source of the intensity and the urgency of their message.

The unity and power discoverable .in the warnings and the promises of the prophets spring from their unwavering conviction that the living God is active in judgment and mercy. His righteous rule is over all nations and all leaders of nations. He requires justice and kindness in the community of his people.

As messengers of the mind of God, the prophets condemned the pride of men (Ezek. 28:2–7), the abuse of economic power (Amos 2:6–7; Mic. 2:1–9), the imperfections and sins of religious leaders (Mic. 3:1–6), and dependence upon military weapons.

> Woe to those who go down to Egypt for help
>   and rely on horses,
> who trust in chariots because they are many
>   and in horsemen because they are very strong.
> but do not look to the Holy One of Israel
>   or consult the Lord!
> And yet he is wise and brings disaster,
>   he does not call back his words,
> but will arise against the house of the evildoers,
>   and against the helpers of those who work
>   iniquity.
>   —Isaiah 31:1–2, RSV

The prophets identified and passed judgment upon the particular sins of men and women, such as pride, greed, dishonesty, theft, adultery, and murder. At crucial moments in perilous times they declared that crime follows crime and that there is no truth or knowledge of God in the land (Jer. 5:26; 7:9–10; Hos. 4:1–2; Amos 8:5–6; Mic. 3:11).

Yet the prophets retained faith in God, who is able to create community among men. And they continued to plead with people to seek justice and righteousness and to be compassionate and faithful to God and his purposes.

The great prophets of Israel spoke with remarkable freedom and courage. Under a sense of divine appointment, they did not hesitate to speak to the nation as a whole or to the king. They made no attempt to reduce what they had to say to what their listeners wanted to hear. They spoke what they firmly believed was God's message to his people at that place and at that time. Nevertheless, there is a timeless element in their message. Their faith in God and their concern for justice were vital forces in ancient Israel and call us to the deepest source of strength in our own day.

The entire message of the Bible in its intention and substance, in its continuity and discontinuity, is a religious message.—It is addressed to the people of God. It is addressed to men of the first century and of subsequent centuries, including the twentieth century. It is addressed to scientists, but it is not a textbook of science and is not to be read as a scientific treatise. It is addressed to creative writers, but it is not a textbook of prose or poetry and is not to be read primarily for a knowledge of its literary forms. It is addressed to preachers, but it is not a textbook of homiletics. It is addressed to historians, but it is not a textbook of history and is not to be read as a technical treatise on history. It is a religious book, and it is to be read for a knowledge of God—who he is, what he has done and said, what he expects and requires of his people, how they are related to him, to one another, and to the world, and what they are to be, say, and do as his children.

The religious character of the biblical writings is explicit throughout the Bible and is discernible with perfect clarity in Jesus Christ. He revealed and obeyed the will of God in a concrete historical situation. In him God's promises to Israel were fulfilled and redemption was wrought. We are saved by the grace of God in Jesus Christ.

What are the implications of the religious nature of the biblical message for the study of the Bible today?

We read the Bible in a mood of expectancy. We are in contact with knowledge about God, and we may come into an encounter with God. We do not know in advance where the religious message of the Bible will become genuinely alive to our minds, and we cannot predict what God will say to us in the encounter.

This means that reading the Bible with a teachable mind is profoundly personal and adventurous. It is somewhat like a journey into a new land. It is a journey which includes a departure, an encounter on the way, and a destiny. The encounter is the great moment in which a person really hears the voice of God for himself and responds in faith or in rebellion.

We read the Bible with the knowledge that its message is to be taken seriously. This is one reason a large number of people disregard the Bible. They do not want to grapple with religious and moral

ideals. One person has said that he decided not to read the Bible
because there is no humor in it. He stated further that Greek thinkers
sometimes made a laughingstock of the gods, but that the Hebrew
thinkers were reverent in the presence of God. There is an element of
truth in his observation. The writers of the Bible were dealing with
religious realities which are to be taken seriously.

This does not mean, however, that there is no joy in the message
of the Bible. Indeed, the deepening of the intellectual and spiritual life
by an affirmative response to God's Word is the source of durable
happiness. Although the word "laughter" is found only 9 times in the
Revised Standard Version, the word "joy" is used 168 times. The
word "gladness" is employed 48 times, the word "glad" is used 90
times, and the word "blessed" occurs 284 times. The word "blessed"
is used in two different senses: it is applied to God and to men.
"Blessed be the Lord" means that God is worthy of adoration. The
word "blessed" applied to men has a variety of meanings, one of
which is "happy" in the original sense of the word in English.
Blessedness is a quality of well-being and genuine happiness in man's
life.

In the preface to the King James Version, the translators referred to manifold blessings, mercies, and happy memories, and
added:

> **But among all our joys, there was no one that more filled our
> hearts, than the blessed continuance of the preaching of God's
> sacred Word among us; which is that inestimable treasure, which
> excelleth all the riches of the earth; because the fruit thereof ex-
> tendeth itself, not only to the time spent in this transitory world,
> but directeth and disposeth men unto that eternal happiness which
> is above in heaven.**

If we read the Bible intelligently in this new day, as a long line of able
and devoted men have done across the years, its message will enable
us not only to endure life but also to enjoy it.

We read the Bible with the awareness that we are to respond to
what God is saying to us. The Bible is God's Word to man through
the medium of human personality in historical contexts. As we learn
what he was saying to and through the Hebrew prophets, and su-
premely in Jesus Christ, we discover that he is speaking to this
generation and to our own minds and hearts. He is calling us to
repentance, to acceptance of the good news that he was in Christ
reconciling the world unto himself, to an understanding of the mind

of Christ as the key to a knowledge of the Scriptures and a coherent interpretation of life, and to a sincere and undivided obedience to God's will. As we walk with Jesus of Nazareth to Jerusalem and to the cross, we discover that the gospel is indeed the power of God unto salvation. We find that it holds a vital and urgent message for us because of its purpose: "that ye might believe that Jesus is the Christ, the Son of God; and that believing ye might have life through his name" (John 20:31).

This brings us to the center of the purpose and message of the Bible: (1) that its readers might be brought near to God; (2) that they might hear God's word and repent of their sins; (3) that their lives might be remade by the power of the gospel; (4) that they might take their places humbly and gratefully in the fellowship of believers; (5) that they might devote their intelligence and energy to tasks in harmony with the mind of Christ. In this generation, when we read the Bible with intellectual understanding and spiritual receptiveness, we acknowledge God's claim upon our lives, open our hearts to him, and identify ourselves with his purposes.

The Message of the Bible Can Be Understood by Christians.

We recognize, of course, that our ability to learn is limited, that our knowledge of the Bible is incomplete, and that the riches of Christ are inexhaustible. At the same time, we acknowledge an aspiration and a responsibility to participate in a systematic and thorough study of the Bible in the days and months immediately ahead.

The intelligibility of the Scriptures to the mind of the thoughtful and devout layman was vigorously affirmed at the time of the Reformation.[1]—Although the reading of the Bible by every Christian was encouraged in the ancient church, the Bible was later withdrawn from the laymen and was read and interpreted by ecclesiastical authorities. In the sixteenth century, however, the unconditional right of every person to read and study the Bible was firmly established and, for the most part, has been maintained.

In order for Christian laymen to grasp the message of the Bible and to guide their lives by it, the Old and New Testaments are translated from the original tongues into many different languages. For example, the translation of the Bible into German by Martin

---

[1] *Encyclopaedia of Religion and Ethics*, ed. James Hastings (New York: Charles Scribner's Sons ,1913), II, 608.

Luther, which appeared in 1534, was an attempt to make the Scriptures available in idiomatic German and, according to Roland H. Bainton, this was "Luther's noblest achievement." [2] This vigorous translation of the Bible released a powerful religious impulse into German life and literature.

The Bible has been translated into hundreds of languages and dialects and is available to millions of individuals around the world. The scholarly work on the text, translation, and distribution of the Bible goes on. The intention of this devoted labor, however, is not fulfilled until persons read the Bible or hear it read, understand the significance of its message, and respond to the grace and truth of God disclosed in it.

The Bible, available in excellent translations, is to be read in its entirety.—The book becomes more intelligible to the person who exposes his mind to its message as a whole and then studies selected books, themes, personalities, and words of the Bible intensively. This is the purpose for the plan of study recommended in an earlier chapter. This is a good time for you to decide to expose yourself afresh to the total message of the Bible. Begin with the four Gospels and read the entire Bible at the rate of about one hundred pages per week for approximately thirteen weeks. You can conserve the results of your personal reading of the Bible by the use of a loose-leaf notebook divided into six sections as suggested on page 107.

The message of the Bible, which is addressed to men in the twentieth century as well as to men in earlier centuries, becomes understandable to us as we read its pages in the search for God's word to us in our own time. This writer became aware of this process of Bible study the summer he was twelve years old. He listened to two series of sermons in which the preachers stressed the severity of God's judgment and rarely mentioned God's mercy. After reflection upon what he had heard, he asked his father, "What did Jesus think and teach about God?" His father gave him a copy of the New Testament in which the teachings of Jesus were printed in red letters and said, "You can learn for yourself what Jesus thought and said about God. Take this New Testament, read his words printed in red, and think about them." This instruction was followed. Every reference to God in the teachings of Jesus was located and pondered, including the prayers. Within a few days the answer was clear: Jesus thought of

---

[2] Roland H. Bainton, *Here I Stand* (New York: Abingdon Press, 1950), p. 326.

God and taught his disciples to think of him not as an enemy but as a friend. This biblical assurance that God knows us as we are and loves us became a firm foundation on which to stand and a beacon to illuminate the path of life.

The Message of the Bible Is Relevant to Decision-Making.

The Bible guides the growth of persons toward mature manhood or womanhood. A careful study of biblical thought equips a person to speak intelligently about the religious dimension of moral issues and to make wise decisions.

In a penetrating article entitled "Toward Maturity in Decision-Making," James M. Gustafson draws attention to the need for mature men in this immature world to participate in discussions of moral issues. Unless we are able to think clearly, to speak precisely, and to evaluate data competently, our voices will not be heard where major decisions are made.

In contemporary American society, as in ancient Israel, life or death depends upon the ability to make wise decisions. The definition of "wisdom" is an exceptionally complicated task, but the meaning of the word as it is used by biblical writers is quite clear. Wisdom is a particular kind of knowledge and skill. It is knowledge of the principles of right action and skill in making thought result in right action. It is the capacity of a godly man to see clearly, to distinguish things that differ, to evaluate data by appropriate criteria, and to approve what is excellent.

In order to make wise personal decisions, a Christian needs a disciplined mind, adequate knowledge of the pertinent data, an appraisal of methods by which the decision is to be implemented, an analysis of predictable consequences, and a capacity to see the issue in the perspective of the mind of Christ. This is the kind of thinking by which a man of mature faith discovers the vocation to which he belongs according to the plan of God and in which he can become a competent workman.

In the formation of a wise group decision, a Christian participates in a thoughtful process. This process may be carried on in the intimacy of the family, in a church, in a community, or in a vocation. It may be carried on in a hospital, for example, where a decision is made by a group of professional persons to transplant or not to transplant a human organ. The leader in the deliberative process may be a Christian surgeon. He will have an enlightened concern for the dignity and worth of every person involved in the decision which he received directly or indirectly from the message of the Bible concerning God and man. He will remember the *Principles of Medical Ethics,* published by the American Medical Association in 1957, including the affirmation that "physicians should strive continually to improve medical knowledge and skill, and should make available to their patients and colleagues the benefits of their professional attainments." [3] In addition to these controlling principles, his thinking will be in harmony with agreed upon guidelines. If the decision involves the transplanting of a heart, he may require (1) that the patient have irreversible cardiac disease, (2) that the disease be untreatable, and (3) that the disease be in its end stages.[4] He will give equal deliberation to the moral and ethical problems related to the heart donor, also. The pertinent data will be evaluated in consultation with colleagues, and the final decision will be the product of the precise and competent work of qualified persons.

The influence of biblical thought upon the decision may not be clearly spelled out by those making the decision, but it will be present and profound. Today only a few Christian thinkers, if any, are adequately prepared to make clear the biblical message concerning life and death. This is a dramatic but undeniable evidence of the need for further study of the sources and relevance of Christian thought to wise decisions in our culture.

Across the centuries Jesus joined hands with the prophets in the insistence upon wise decisions. He made personal decisions. He selected disciples with utmost care (Luke 6:12–13). He taught them to think for themselves. He drew attention to pertinent data concerning urgent issues, and he exercised skill in guiding the thinking of the disciples to valid conclusions, wise decisions, and firm commitments (Luke 14:1 to 21:38). He marked out with clarity and precision the path which leads to maturity in the decision-making process. This type of maturity is characterized by respect for all discoverable facts, honesty in the evaluation of the facts, readiness to listen thoughtfully to competent interpreters of criteria and data, skill in the direction of thought to major aspects of an issue, capacity to express a decision coherently, and courage to accept responsibility for the consequences.

---

[3] *Principles of Medical Ethics* (Chicago: American Medical Association, 1957), Section 2.
[4] *Winston-Salem Journal,* September 28, 1968, p. 1.

In the Message of the Bible We Find Guidance and Incentive for Right Action in Practical Situations.

We learn that right action emerges out of wise decision, is measured by the plumb line of justice, and is motivated by love.

In a search for the source and direction of right action, consider the following seven passages of the Bible for intensive study. This selection of passages and books of the Bible provides a broad basis for an examination of the vital interrelation of religious faith and moral rectitude.

> The Ten Commandments (Ex. 20:1–17)
> A summary of what God requires of man (Mic. 6:8)
> The book of Amos
> The Sermon on the Mount (Matt. 5:1 to 7:27) *
> The letter of Paul to the Ephesians *
> The letter of Paul to the Romans *
> The primacy of love (Mark 12:28–31)

In addition to three summaries of religious and moral insights, this selection of biblical documents includes the Sermon on the Mount and three books of the Bible. An adequate study of this collection of biblical writings will be exacting in its demands but rewarding in its results. *It is recommended that, in addition to your regular schedule of Bible study in Sunday School, you devote approximately two hours per week for a year to this study.* It is recommended, further, that you examine with very great care the major themes, the key words, and the central ideas expressed in this group of writings, using the tools of biblical scholarship outlined in chapter 2 of this book and recording the results of your study and reflection in a notebook. If you undertake, continue, and complete this study, you will have a profound knowledge of religious faith and right conduct. The task recommended calls for heroic effort. You can do it.

To deal competently and constructively with the urgent issues of our time, we must consider specific questions and complex problems with a clear understanding of the way of life set forth in the total message of the Bible. A study of the passages above will help to provide that understanding.

In the Bible life is portrayed as a pilgrimage, a struggle, and a victory. You may decide to begin this study of the way of life set forth in this selection of biblical writings by a preliminary and rapid

---

* Study guides for these sections appear on pages 162-68 of this book.

reading of the material, with attention to the following clues to an understanding of the message:

God is the ultimate source of our knowledge of right action.— He spoke the words which were recorded in the Ten Commandments. He has shown us what is good. His righteous rule is over all nations. We are to seek first his kingdom and his righteousness. He disclosed his love for us in Jesus Christ, and we are to love him with mind, heart, soul, and strength.

Right action is defined by what God requires of men and not primarily in terms of what men seek for themselves. A central question is, "What doth the Lord require of thee?" Every page in the above selection of biblical material is related directly or indirectly to this question. Amos, for example, insisted that the righteous God requires justice in the personal, economic, and political life of his people; and he demonstrates the nature and practice of justice.

On the human pilgrimage, a man who lives by faith in God and his moral requirements has compassion and enlightened concern for the well-being of every individual he meets.—He has a high regard for the dignity and worth of man. He speaks the truth to his companions. He loves his neighbor, and in his best moments he knows that every man is his neighbor. He seeks justice for his neighbor. He understands that we are members one of another. It is right for us to help and not to hurt one another, to encourage and not to discourage one another, to be kind and not cruel to one another.

A man of Christian faith must examine each life situation in the light of the mind of Christ.—A study of the Sermon on the Mount and Paul's letter to the Romans will help you gain insight into the mind of our Lord. The Sermon on the Mount throws a flood of light on the realities with which the Christian wrestles in daily living. As A. M. Hunter has said, "Christ calls us to the adventure of Christian living, sets before us a pattern of life, and tells us who God is, the kind of people we ought to be, and the attitudes we should manifest toward God and toward one another." [5]

Guided by the insights presented in the recommended biblical studies, we discover the **direction** *of right action.*—We can base our sense of direction on moral instruction in Romans 12–14 and Ephesians 4–6. This instruction can be used constructively in the situations in which we make decisions and take action today. For example, what

[5] A. M. Hunter, *Pattern for Life* (London: SCM Press Ltd., 1953), pp. 113–15.

is deeply characteristic of the action of a Christian driver of an automobile on a modern highway? He operates the machine with knowledge and skill derived not from the Bible but from technology. He performs his function as a driver in harmony with legal requirements which have been translated into traffic regulations. Beyond these technical and legal considerations, he has an attitude of goodwill toward every person he meets or passes on the highway. This attitude is an expression of compassion for the neighbor which is in harmony with the way of life described in the biblical writings. He truly loves God and is personally committed to Jesus Christ as Saviour and Lord. Although he is limited by many factors and makes mistakes, he is a competent, courteous, Christian driver.

In the fellowship of believers, love motivates right action in all relationships.—In the vertical relation of man to God, love is expressed in trust in God's goodness, reverence for God's wisdom, and obedience to God's will. In the horizontal relation of man to his neighbor, love is expressed in acceptance and understanding of the neighbor as a person, appreciation of his dignity and worth, and an attitude of goodwill toward him. When we render competent service motivated by love, we are doing for our neighbors something of what God has already done for us in Jesus Christ: We love them as he has loved us. We forgive them as he has forgiven us. We take costly action in their behalf as he has taken costly action in our behalf.

In the effort to relate biblical truth to the decision-making process and the action which issues out of it, it is helpful for us to remember the *permeability* of man (penetrable), the *malleability* of social structures (the ability to be shaped or molded), and the *responsibility* of Christian men and women. Man as a human being and as a believer has a capacity to open his mind to truth, to companions, to the Holy Spirit. He understands how little he knows, and how little his neighbors know, about the fundamental issues of life and death, about justice and love, about sin and forgiveness, about hope and fulfilment. This recognition of the limits of knowledge is akin to the humility of a teachable mind. It creates readiness to receive insight at the great moments of encounter with God and man in the process of human growth. At one of the teachable moments in his growth toward maturity, man discerns that social structures are made by men and can be changed by men. The institutions and agencies within a community are formed by men and can be reformed by men. Political parties, economic systems, and international relations are formed by men and can be reformed by men. It is the responsibility of Christian men and women to participate in the needful work of the world, in the processes through which decisions are made, and in the interpretation and reformation of social structures. "Where there is no vision, the people perish" (Prov. 29:18). "Blessed are the pure in heart: for they shall see God" (Matt. 5:8).

The strength of men and of nations does not reside exclusively in physical resources, scientific skill, and technological advancement. It is renewed by men and women who have confidence in the power of truth, who read the Bible with understanding, who participate in wise decisions and right action, and who face an unrevealed future with the assurance that nothing can separate them from the love of God in Jesus Christ.

Additional Enrichment Resources

Building Your Own Resources—*Richard Kornmeyer*
How to Use a Bible Commentary and Dictionary—*Ralph McLain*
Archaeology and the Bible—*Edgar McKnight*
Explore It—*Robert A. Baker*

Outlines for Bible Study

THE SERMON ON THE MOUNT—*Robert A. Dean*
ROMANS—*Robert A. Dean*
EPHESIANS—*Charles Treadway*

Building Your Own Resources [1]

Compiled by Richard Kornmeyer

Bible

Bridges, Ronald, and Weigle, Luther. *The Bible Word Book*. New York: Thomas Nelson and Sons, 1960.

Containing 827 articles concerning words in the King James Version which have been affected by changing English usage, this book is addressed to the general reader. It explains what the King James translators meant by these words, and what words replace them in modern translations.

Brooks, D. P. *The Bible—How to Understand and Teach It*. Nashville: Broadman Press, 1969.

This book deals with the nature of the Bible—problems in understanding it, approaches to understanding it, how to learn to better interpret the Bible, and ways to explain it to others.

Cartledge, Samuel A. *The Bible: God's Word to Man*. Nashville: Broadman Press, 1961.

This book seeks to give some insight into the nature of the Bible and to acquaint the reader with the many areas of biblical scholarship that can aid him in coming to a richer, fuller understanding of the meaning of the Bible.

Deal, William S. *Baker's Pictorial Introduction to the Bible*. Grand Rapids: Baker Book House, 1967.

The theme of this book is an acknowledgment that a sovereign God lives and acts today. It provides concise information about each of the sixty-six books of the Bible, aiding in a better understanding of who wrote each book, when each was written, and the particular circumstances surrounding its writing.

Demaray, Donald E. *A Layman's Guide to Our Bible*. Grand Rapids: Zondervan Publishing House, 1964.

The purpose of this handbook is to provide ready information about the Bible. It is divided into three parts, each having three chapters: (1) Our Bible: Charting Its Course; (2) Our Bible: Book by Book; (3) Our Bible: Persons, Places, Things.

---

[1] The listing of these books does not necessarily imply endorsement of their total content by author or publisher.

One appendix offers bibliographical suggestions for further study of the Bible.

Halley, Henry H. *Halley's Bible Handbook.* Grand Rapids: Zondervan Publishing House, 1965.

There is probably more biblical information available here than in any other book of its size. The user will find an abbreviated Bible commentary, an atlas of seventy-five maps, a concise church history, archaeological notes, and the story of the miraculous chain of events through which the Bible was written and preserved for all mankind.

Johnson, L. D. *An Introduction to the Bible.* Nashville: Convention Press, 1969.

This book was written to tell what kind of book the Bible is, how it came together, what its unifying themes are, and what it says to us today. This is Volume 1 in the Bible Survey Series.

McKnight, Edgar V. *Opening the Bible.* Nashville: Broadman Press, 1967.

This guide to the understanding of the Scriptures deals with the people and culture of the Bible lands and the history of God's people. Principles for Bible study are given that are practical for the average layman.

Newman, Barclay M. *The Meaning of the New Testament.* Nashville: Broadman Press, 1966.

The author surveys the New Testament by discussing the content and purpose of each book, as well as background matters. He gives more attention to the messages of the books than most works of this type.

Perry, Lloyd M., and Culver, Robert D. *How to Search the Scriptures.* Grand Rapids: Baker Book House, 1967.

This book gives guidance in about every imaginable way to study the Bible. Methods are given for studying the Bible by books, chapters, paragraphs, parts of Scripture, doctrine, biographies, prayers, miracles, parables, poetry, and writers.

Smith, Wilbur M. *Profitable Bible Study.* Natick, Massachusetts: W. A. Wilde Co., 1963.

The author sets forth seven great things the study of the Bible will do for us and eight methods for studying the Bible for our own soul's nourishment. The second part of the book is a bibliography of literature on the Bible.

Ward, Wayne E. *The Word Comes Alive*. Nashville: Broadman Press, 1969.

This guide to Bible interpretation was written to show the serious Bible reader how to discover the message of the Bible in greater depth and how to communicate it to others more effectively.

Watts, James W. *Old Testament Teaching*. Nashville: Broadman Press, 1967.

The purpose of this study is to guide students of the Bible to those viewpoints from which they may continue Old Testament interpretation independently.

Bible Biography

Deen, Edith. *All of the Women of the Bible*. New York: Harper & Row, 1955.

An exhaustive collection of biographies of women mentioned in the Scriptures. The author has attempted to re-create those women so that they might be seen as real human beings and to interpret their spiritual experiences, their faith, and their relationship with God.

Lockyer, Herbert. *All the Men of the Bible*. Grand Rapids: Zondervan Publishing House, 1958.

As a biographical dictionary, this very useful volume will be a ready helper for Bible students. Names are listed alphabetically, their meanings are given, and all biblical references are listed.

Bible Commentaries

Davidson, Francis (ed.). *The New Bible Commentary*. Grand Rapids: William B. Eerdmans Publishing Co., 1953.

Based on the careful study of fifty Bible scholars, this commentary is fresh and makes the text of the Bible plain to the average reader in its introductions, outlines, and commentaries on every book of the Bible.

Pfeiffer, Charles F., and Harrison, Everett F. (eds.). *The Wycliffe Bible Commentary*. Chicago: Moody Press, 1962.

This is, strictly speaking, neither a devotional nor a technical exegetical treatment. It seeks to present the biblical message in such a way that the serious Bible student will find extensive help within its pages.

Bible Concordances

Cruden, Alexander. *Cruden's Unabridged Concordance to the Old and New Testaments.* Grand Rapids: Baker Book House, 1953.

This concordance includes a collection of the names and titles given to Jesus Christ, an alphabetical table of the proper names in the Scriptures and their meaning, a concordance to these proper names, and a compendium of each chapter of the Bible.

Nave, Orville J. *Nave's Topical Bible.* Chicago: Moody Press.

Almost all that the Bible teaches about twenty thousand different subjects can be found in this book. All verses on a particular subject are brought together under a topical heading, and the headings are listed alphabetically throughout the book. Most of the passages are written out rather than only listed as references. Verses having the same idea are also included. It is this reference that makes this book more valuable than a regular concordance.

Bible Dictionaries

Douglas, James D. (ed.). *The New Bible Dictionary.* Grand Rapids: William B. Eerdmans Publishing Co., 1962.

This is an exhaustive dictionary of biblical names, subjects, places, and so on. It gives a more thorough treatment than do most one-volume dictionaries. The historical development of a particular subject, doctrine, or concept is traced. It treats a greater variety of subjects than do most Bible dictionaries.

Tenney, Merrill C. (ed.). *The Zondervan Pictorial Bible Dictionary.* Grand Rapids: Zondervan Publishing House, 1963.

This one-volume dictionary features illustrative materials along with the article on the same subject. A full complement of charts and maps adds to the usefulness of this work.

Bible Geography and History

Adams, J. McKee. *Biblical Backgrounds.* Revised by Joseph Callaway. Nashville: Broadman Press, 1965.

This survey of Bible geography and history gives the setting for the major events of the Old and New Testaments. Sixteen pages of colored maps, numerous smaller black and white maps, and seventy full-page photographs make the study of biblical geography more attractive.

Grollenberg, Lucas H. *Shorter Atlas of the Bible.* New York: Thomas Nelson and Sons, 1959.

Presented in a concise form is a picture of the world in which the books of the Bible found their origin. The author has presented maps, a large number of illustrations, and a short text to link them together.

May, Herbert G. (ed.). *Oxford Bible Atlas*. New York: Oxford University Press, 1962.

In all the maps of this atlas the Bible is central; and their purpose is to throw light on it and to relate it to its historical and geographical setting. This is basically an atlas of maps with accompanying text.

Pfeiffer, Charles (ed.). *Baker's Bible Atlas*. Nashville: Broadman Press, 1961.

The content of this atlas is organized to follow the scriptural narrative, making it readily usable as a Bible study aid. In addition to twenty-six colored maps, each chapter has its black and white outline maps showing clearly the geographic features emphasized in that chapter. Photographs illustrate and illuminate the text.

Pfeiffer, Charles, and Vos, Howard. *The Wycliffe Historical Geography of Bible Lands*. Chicago: Moody Press, 1967.

The authors have brought together historical, geographical, biblical, and archaeological material on all ten areas of the Near Eastern and Mediterranean world that might properly be called "Bible lands."

Bible Harmonies

Carter, John F. *A Layman's Harmony of the Gospels*. Nashville: Broadman Press, 1961.

The outstanding feature of this book is the extensive body of notes, running almost commentary-style along with the text. They include information on dates and history, interpretation of difficult passages, and explanation of customs of the times.

Crockett, William D. *A Harmony of the Books of Samuel, Kings, and Chronicles*. Grand Rapids: Baker Book House, 1951.

The author "harmonizes" the six books noted in the title by placing their accounts of the same event in parallel columns.

Goodwin, Frank J. *A Harmony of the Life of St. Paul*. Grand Rapids: Baker Book House, 1964.

The author has constructed a continuous account of the life

of Paul as given in Acts, together with such selections from the
Pauline Epistles as are supplementary or parallel.

Robertson, A. T. *A Harmony of the Gospels for Students of the Life
of Christ*. New York: Harper & Row, 1922.

The four Gospels are arranged chronologically in parallel columns for easy comparison. Outlines, tables, lists, and additional
notes are also included to assist the student in studying the life of
Christ.

Biblical Archaeology

Pfeiffer, Charles (ed.). *The Biblical World*. Grand Rapids: Baker
Book House, 1966.

This book is claimed to be the first dictionary for the Bible
student on biblical archaeology. Numerous photographs illustrate
the text.

Vardaman, E. Jerry. *Archaeology and the Living Word*. Nashville:
Broadman Press, 1965.

The author gives an account of excavation methods, then deals
with notable Old and New Testament discoveries and their relation
to Bible stories and personalities.

Wright, George E. *Biblical Archaeology*. Philadelphia: Westminster
Press, 1963.

In this revised and expanded edition, the author has sought to
bring up to date his earlier presentation. New sections describe
how the histories of some of the most important cities of ancient
Israel must be rewritten.

How to Use a Bible Commentary and Dictionary [1]

Ralph McLain

The psalmist wrote, "I prevented the dawning of the morning" (Psalm 119:147). Can it be "prevented" today? Easily, if one knows what "prevent" meant in A.D. 1611, when the King James Version was published. But the modern reader needs help.

One of Jesus' parables begins: "What woman having ten pieces of silver, if she lose one piece, doth not light a candle, and sweep the house, and seek diligently till she find it?" (Luke 15:8). Why did she look so hard? Was she poor? No. Was the piece valuable? No. The clue lies in the phrase "having *ten* pieces." We need help to interpret it.

The Sunday School lesson for a given Sunday may be about "the call of Abraham." Does "call" mean "shout"? Hardly! "Call" in Latin is *voco* from which the word "vocation" comes. Most of us think "vocation" is one's work. This was not the original meaning. What does it mean? Again, help is needed.

Further, the Scripture passage for this Sunday School lesson would include the phrase, "And make thy name great" (Gen. 12:2). "Abram" in big neon letters? Hardly that! The clue lies in the word "name," which was a profound word. We do not "name" people the way the ancients did.

Answers to such questions can be found in Bible commentaries. The purpose of this article is to help the Bible student understand what Bible commentaries, concordances, and dictionaries are and how to use them.

COMMENTARIES

A devoted, though untrained, elderly woman received a Bible commentary as a Christmas present. She wrote, thanking the donor, and added: "It's a nice book, but it's a good thing there is a Scripture reference at the top of the page to explain all the print at the bottom of the page!" She may have had a point. Nevertheless, many sincere Bible students have received remarkable help from commentaries.

What is a commentary? It is a book of comments on the words

[1] Ralph McLain, *Young People Training for Action*, October–December, 1966, pp. 28–32. Reproduced by permission. Dr. McLain is professor of religion at Meredith College, Raleigh, North Carolina.

and thoughts of the Bible or a portion of the Bible. Usually, the Bible verses appear or are indicated at the top of the page. The rest of the page is written to explain the Scripture references, verse by verse.

Many church members have never seen a commentary. A page from *The Wycliffe Bible Commentary* is reproduced on page 146.

Look at this reproduction. Circle the number of the Bible verses. Draw a box around the comments.

Read the reproduction, noting information you gained which you perhaps would not have obtained by reading the Scripture passage alone.

In addition to verse-by-verse comments, most commentaries have introductions to each Bible book and some introductory articles such as "History of Israel," "Life of Jesus," "Miracles," "Biblical Archaeology," "The Formation of the Bible," and "Doctrines in the New Testament." At the end of most commentaries there is usually a set of maps, occasionally a glossary of Bible words, and other helps.

Who writes commentaries? Seldom does one man feel capable of writing a commentary on the entire Bible. Scholars usually specialize in one area of Bible study. Therefore, a complete commentary may be the work of many scholars.* One man usually edits the commentary; many men contribute to it. For instance, a commentary produced in the United States in recent years is the twelve-volume set *The Interpreter's Bible*. Well over one hundred and fifty scholars of America and England contributed material in the field of their speciality.

How does one choose a commentary? Here are some guidelines.

1. Be sure that the commentary is published by a good publishing house and that the authors are competent Christian scholars. Realize that, in sets of books, some are better than others. Many scholars never buy whole sets. They choose the best books from different sets.

2. Realize that some commentaries are scholarly; some are more popular in approach. Therefore, personal preference is also a factor in selection.

3. Decide which you can afford. There are several good one-volume commentaries which are relatively inexpensive. There are many multiple-volume commentaries.

4. Be sure the type is easy to read.

---

* Editor's note: *The Broadman Bible Commentary* is now available and will provide excellent study help for the serious Bible student. Consult a Baptist Book Store.

CONCORDANCES

A very practical aid to Bible study is the concordance. A concordance is a book listing alphabetically the words used in the Bible. With each word is a list of verses in which the word is used. For instance, in *Cruden's Complete Concordance*, under *l* the word "love" is given, with every place it occurs in the Bible from Genesis to Revelation. Including its combination in phrases, such as "love of God," it is listed over two hundred and fifty times.

Why are there different concordances? Every version of the Bible must have its own concordance, because each one uses at least slightly different wording. For example, the word "straightway" in the King James Version (1611) is often translated "immediately" in more recent versions. The meaning is the same; the words are different. There is usually at least one concordance for each new version of the Bible.

Modern technology has changed concordance-making. Until recently, concordances were done by many people working over a long time, laboriously listing each word in each place it occurred in the Bible and then alphabetizing the lists. It took thirty years to make *Cruden's Complete Concordance*. *Nelson's Complete Concordance of the Revised Standard Version Bible* was made by a computer in four hundred hours.

How is a concordance used? The simplest use of the concordance is that of helping one locate Scripture references. Suppose one says: "I have heard of a verse that goes something like 'God loved the world that he gave his Son. . . .' I can't remember it exactly, and I don't know where it is."

The concordance will help. Pick out a word, for example "loved." Look under the *l*'s until you find "loved." Look down the column of phrases taken from the entire Bible. You will come to one that reads "God so *l.* the world." By that phrase will be "John 3:16."

How is a concordance to be used? The most readily available concordances are the abbreviated ones in the backs of many Bibles. If you have such a Bible, turn to the concordance, locate and "trace" the following words, and list some of the other places where these words appear in the Bible:

1. bondage
2. Passover

3. lintel

4. firstborn

A common use of a concordance is to trace a word through the Bible. (There are also topical textbooks which trace principal topics or ideas through the Bible.)

The process of tracing a word is simple. The concordance lists the references so that one need only find one after the other. Reading the passages together may give understanding that a separate reading of each verse has not given.

DICTIONARIES

The Bible dictionary is one of the most helpful books one can add to his library. In one volume there is competent helpfulness covering the whole Bible.

The meaning of the term is obvious because everyone is acquainted with dictionaries. The method of locating entries is obvious: Entries are arranged alphabetically. The content is not so obvious. The only words in a Bible dictionary are words that occur in the Bible. For instance, the words "choir," "creed," and "Sunday School" do not occur in *Harper's Bible Dictionary*. They are not biblical words. Also, the meaning given is that which the word had in its biblical use.

The entries resemble those of an encyclopedia in their descriptions and scope. Accompanying these word descriptions are many interesting pictures and maps.

On page 146 is a facsimile of a Bible dictionary entry. Read it as you study your Sunday School lesson for next Sunday.

List one commentary, one concordance, and one dictionary which you would like to own. Head this list "Christmas and Birthday Gift Suggestions." Keep it handy for use by family and friends!

"I always examine a man's library. He may conceal himself from me in social niceties, but the curtain is pulled aside when I see his library." The man who spoke these words obviously knew both books and men. If what he said is true of men and books in general, is it not true also of Christians and their Bible-study books? A Christian's concern for growth in biblical understanding will be reflected by his library.

4) The Law of the Manna. 8:1–20.

The focal point of this chapter is verse 17, with its picture of a future Israel at ease in Canaan, basking in self-congratulation. The recollection of God's providential guidance during the forty years in the wilderness (v. 2 ff.) would afford the corrective for such vanity.

1–6. Verse 1 is another introductory summary of the covenant summons and sanctions (see also 4:1; 5:1; 6:1). **2.** So far as the surviving generation was concerned, the wilderness wandering was designed as a period of probation—**to prove thee**—(v. 2b; cf. 13:3) and of necessary instruction (v. 3c). It was a fatherly discipline and contributed to their ultimate blessing (v. 5; cf. 16c). **3. He . . . fed thee with manna.** What is meant by God's humbling Israel (v. 2) is illustrated by reference to his extraordinary provision for every need during the forty years (vv. 3,4; cf. 29:5,6), particularly by means of the manna (see Ex. 16, esp. v. 4). Humbling consisted of privation and then the provision of the "What-is-it?," the unknown, supernatural bread of heaven, which compelled the people to recognize their dependence on God (cf. Deut. 8:16a,b). Modern natural-

in the Arabah. **11. Beware that thou forget not.** Though all these natural products were to be gratefully recognized as the gifts of God just as much as the supernatural manna (v. 10b), luxury and ease would blunt the edge of Israel's awareness of God (vv. 12,13). **14. Thine heart be lifted up.** Pride would suppress the memory of humbler days of slavery, scorpions, and thirst, days when deliverance and survival required divine intervention by hitherto unknown ways (vv. 15,16). Of such denial of their Lord through self-adulation they must beware. The same truth that had to be learned in the former days of empty stomachs would be the relevant truth in the coming days of full stomachs: the source of man's life is the word of God—**he . . . giveth thee power** (17,18a). Israel's beatitude was due solely to God's fidelity to his covenant oath (v. 18b; cf. Gen. 15). At the same time the Lord would visit upon covenant-breakers the curses they had invoked. **20. So shall ye perish.** Repudiation of election as the Lord's peculiar possession, and identification with the anathematized Canaanites in their idolatrous iniquity, would result in Israel's identification with the

First′-born′ or **First′ling,** the former being used chiefly of men, the latter always of beasts. To the first-born offspring of men and animals God the giver has the first claim (cf. Gen. 4:4). Among the Israelites an additional reason existed in the fact that Jehovah had freed the people from Egyptian bondage. In the 10th and last plague of Egypt the first-born of the Egyptians were slain, while the first-born of the Israelites were preserved by sprinkling blood on the lintels and doorposts of the houses within which they resided (Ex. 12: 12, 13, 23, 29). Saved in this manner, they became consecrated to Jehovah. Every first-born male of man and beast was holy to the Lord (chs. 13:2; 34:19), and could not be used by man (Lev. 27:26), but belonged to the sanctuary for sacrifice; the first-born of man, however, was redeemed (Ex. 13:13, 15; 34:20; cf. Lev. 27:6). On this occasion he was brought to the sanctuary and presented to Jehovah (Luke 2:22; cf. Num. 18:15). The Levites were afterward substituted for the Israelite first-born (Num. 3:12, 41, 46; 8:13–19; cf. Ex. 32:26–29) and served at the sanctuary. Those of animals also, against which

Archaeology and the Bible
Edgar McKnight

Sensational discoveries in Bible lands, such as the Dead Sea scrolls in 1947, have helped to popularize biblical archaeology. These discoveries and the interpretations of them by some have lead some people to think of biblical archaeology as something quite different from what it really is.

WHAT IS BIBLICAL ARCHAEOLOGY?

The term "archaeology" comes from two Greek words (*archaios,* ancient, and *logos,* discourse) and designates the scientific study of the material remains of past life. The field for archaeology is the world. There are special branches for every region of the world, America, South Africa, England, Palestine—wherever men have lived.

Biblical archaeology deals with the lands of the Bible and the material remains which are related to biblical people and events. It is, perhaps, the best known branch of archaeology due to widespread interest in the Bible.

At the outset the purpose and limitations of biblical archaeology should be set forth. Its purpose is not to prove or disprove the Bible. Research has often confirmed specific facts in the Bible record, but archaeologists do not begin with the objective of proving any particular point. The help provided by biblical archaeology is a greater understanding of the times, events, and people recorded in the Bible. It unveils the past and relates it to the biblical narrative. A modern archaeologist says,

> No one can understand the Bible without a knowledge of biblical history and culture, and no one can claim a knowledge of biblical history and culture without an understanding of the contributions of archaeology. Biblical events have been illustrated, obscure words defined, ideas explained, and chronology refined, by archaeological finds. To say that our knowledge of the Bible has been revolutionized by these discoveries is to understate the facts.[1]

"Archaeology and the Bible" is reprinted from *Opening the Bible* (Nashville: Broadman Press, 1967), pp. 109–122 by permission of Broadman Press. Dr. McKnight is assistant professor of religion and classical languages, Furman University, Greenville, South Carolina.

HISTORICAL SKETCH OF BIBLICAL ARCHAEOLOGY

The Bible lands constitute more than the country of Palestine. Egypt, Assyria, Asia Minor, Macedonia, Greece, and even Rome are related to the biblical narrative and constitute a valid interest for biblical archaeology. Palestine is of central interest because it was the land to which the people of Israel came from bondage in Egypt; it was the land of David and Solomon; it was the land of Jesus.

Scientific study of the material remains in the Near East is not old. Before World War I, limited work was done in a very elementary way.

After World War I, the British, with a mandate over Palestine, established a department of antiquities. Excavation was quickly resumed. All the activities in Palestine and the surrounding areas in the period between the two world wars are impossible to catalog here. Developments greatly increased knowledge of the biblical world which in turn enlarged our understanding of the Bible. By comparing the results of work in various areas of the biblical world, a clearer picture of Palestine and the ancient Near East could be formed. W. F. Albright, an outstanding American archaeologist, feels that 1939 was a significant year for biblical archaeology: "The time had come to begin the preparation of real syntheses of ancient Near-Eastern history and civilization." [2] He declared that because knowledge of archaeological chronology had increased so rapidly during the previous decades, events and cultural activities in different lands could now be correctly dated and related to one another.

During and following World War II, archaeological activity continued and increased. Arab-Israeli hostilities stopped excavation in Palestine for a period, but with the ending of hostilities and the partitioning of Palestine, work resumed in Israel and Jordan.

SOME BIBLICAL ARCHAEOLOGY DISCOVERIES

Archaeologists have uncovered a multitude of material objects in biblical lands, and scholars have worked diligently using them to illuminate the Bible and biblical history. Perhaps the most important contributions to our understanding of the Bible have been made through the discovery of certain written documents. Not all of them were brought to light by archaeological excavation; many were discovered by chance. But scholars have cooperated in studying all the documents and applying their knowledge to biblical study.

Babylonian Chronicle.—The Assyrian and Babylonian kings maintained written records of their activities. Since they had important contacts with Israel and Judah during the Old Testament periods, these countries are mentioned in the records kept by the kings. For the neo-Babylonian period an "unusually objective and reliable source" [3] is provided by the "Babylonian Chronicle."

The texts (on clay tablets) were found along with other historical records in the excavated cities of ancient Mesopotamia. The Babylonian Chronicle is important for its contemporary account of activities from about the time of Ashurbanipal's death to the fall of Babylon to Cyrus in 539 B.C.

The Black Obelisk.—What is claimed to be "the most important single monument for illustrating the Bible" [4] as well as the only existing portrait of a king of Israel was discovered in December of 1846 at Nimrud, a mound in ancient Assyria. This monument is the Black Obelisk and contains the annals of Shalmaneser III, a great Assyrian king. Of particular interest is a series of three panels showing Shalmaneser III receiving tribute from the Israelite king Jehu, son of Omri.

Moabite Stone.—In 1868 a European missionary traveling east of the Dead Sea viewed a slab of black basalt. It was discovered to contain an important inscription telling of the wars and constructions of Mesha, king of Moab, in the ninth century B.C. Although the stone was later broken up, a squeeze (a copy made by placing soggy paper on the inscription, which when dry retains an impression of the writing) was made before the destruction. The text tells of relations between Mesha and King Omri of Israel.

Siloam Inscription.—On a hot June day, 1880, a young boy, playing in Jerusalem, waded in a pool of water south of the Old City. He was actually wading in a tunnel long known to archaeologists. Edward Robinson, 42 years earlier, had found that the tunnel was the conduit for water from a spring to the north, and he believed that the tunnel ended in the Pool of Siloam mentioned in the Bible.

The young, native boy slipped into the waters of the stream, and when he came to the surface he noticed some letters cut into the tunnel wall. News of the inscription spread. When scholars translated the writing, the inscription was discovered to be an ancient "plaque" describing the very work mentioned in the Bible (2 Kings 20:20; 2 Chron. 32:30).

Amarna Tablets.—In the fall of 1887, a group of over three hundred clay tablets was found by an Egyptian woman who lived near Tell el Amarna (about two hundred miles south of Cairo). The tablets were sold to a neighbor, who in turn disposed of them for a profit. Eighty-two of the tablets were purchased by the British Museum, but the remainder quickly spread throughout the world. This discovery, with the later discoveries of archaeologists, provided approximately 307 tablets containing Babylonian cuneiform. Cuneiform scholars quickly saw that the tablets constituted a file of the Egyptian foreign office during the reigns of two Egyptian rulers.

These letters are a major source of knowledge concerning the history of Palestine and Syria during the early fourteenth century B.C. for many of the letters are from rulers in important towns in Palestine and Syria.

Code of Hammurabi.—In the last part of 1901 and the first of 1902, three large pieces of stone were discovered at Susa (one-time capital of Elam). When put together, these pieces formed a monument over seven feet high and covered with columns of cuneiform writings and a scene of a king before the sun-god Shamash. This turned out to be a law code of Hammurabi containing about two hundred and fifty laws and dating back to 1792–1750 B.C. Apparently, it had been carried away from Babylon to Susa after the time of Hammurabi.

This code is important as a source for knowledge of Babylonian daily life during the time of the Hebrew patriarchs. James B. Pritchard declares that it "has thrown more light on life in ancient Babylonia than any other single monument." [5]

Execration Texts.—In 1926 a volume was published containing texts from broken pieces of pottery bowls which had been purchased at Thebes in Egypt by the Berlin Museum. The writings on the pottery were "execration texts," curses which apparently were to become effective when the pottery was smashed. On these bowls, and on fragments of clay figurines found later in Egypt, names of rulers, tribes, and cities are mentioned. Some towns mentioned in the Bible are also mentioned in these texts. Perhaps this practice is related to a practice recorded in Jeremiah 19:11–12.

Ras Shamra Discoveries.—In 1928 a Syrian plowman accidentally ran his plow into a large stone and discovered that it belonged to a tomb. This accident led to the discovery of a cemetery and a lost ancient city which is the most important Canaanite site archaeologists have yet found. In May of 1929, a library of the ancient city was discovered. A few days later a number of inscribed tablets were uncovered. They were in an unknown cuneiform script—later deciphered and called Ugarit, after the ancient name of the town where the texts were found.

Ugarit has supplied invaluable materials for an understanding of the religious situation in Canaan before the Israelites came. The documents contain not only religious texts but letters, commercial texts, school work, and legal writings.

Lachish Letters.—The Lachish letters, dating from the time of Jeremiah and addressed to a military officer (probably the commander of Lachish, a town in southern Palestine), were from a subordinate in charge of a northern outpost. The writing was on pottery and in the Hebrew language. The letters indicate the form which Hebrew correspondence took, show how ancient Hebrew characters were formed, and provide insight into the history of the crises years of the 580's B.C.

The letters were found in debris from ancient Lachish. The first one was recognized on January 29, 1935, by some writing on a piece of broken pottery which was in some material from a Persian roadway through a gate to Lachish. By the time all the letters had been discovered (much of the correspondence was never recovered, of course), about a hundred lines of Hebrew writing from the time of Jeremiah had been recovered.

Gnostic Writings.—*The Secret Sayings of Jesus* is a book which promises something special for the followers of Christ. It is an introduction, translation, and commentary on one of a collection of "Gnostic" writings accidentally discovered in 1945 or 1946 about thirty-two miles north of Luxor on the Nile River.

The thirteen codices had been well preserved in jars (perhaps one very large jar), and nearly 80 of the 100 pages of manuscript were intact. The writing is Coptic (apparently a translation from Greek originals) and the materials date to the third or fourth centuries A.D. Twelve of the volumes became the property of the Coptic Museum. One volume was acquired by the Jung Institute in Zurich, Switzerland. This has become known as the Jung Codex and contains "The Gospel of Truth" which was translated in 1956. Later in 1956 another volume was made public by the director of the Coptic

Museum at Cairo. Among other writings, this volume contains "The Gospel of Thomas," which was translated into English in 1958.

NOT EQUAL TO NEW TESTAMENT

These writings show how one early group of Christians understood and reinterpreted Christ. The writings are not on a par with the New Testament writings. They are later reflections on the meaning of Jesus and his message from the point of view of "Gnostics," a religious movement of the second century and later, which emphasized "knowledge [gnosis]" as a means of redemption.

Dead Sea Scrolls.—The Dead Sea scrolls currently are the center of attention in the minds of most people. These scrolls were discovered in 1947 when an Arab shepherd accidentally found several manuscripts in a cave on the west shore of the Dead Sea. They eventually became the possession of the State of Israel, but because of the war between the Arabs and the Israeli, a scientific investigation of the cave area was delayed. When an investigation was made early in 1949, several hundred fragments of biblical and nonbiblical writings were found.

Since then more scrolls and fragments have been found in the caves around the area, and nearby ruins that have been excavated show that the site was a large monastery which served as a center for a Jewish group living in the area.

Scholarly discussions have taken place on such questions as the date of the scrolls and the identification of the group which used them. By various means scholars have determined that the group was a segment of the Essenes (one of the major Jewish groups of New Testament times, discussed by Philo, Josephus, and Pliny) and that the scrolls date to the first century A.D. and earlier.

The Dead Sea scrolls are important for a number of reasons. The Old Testament manuscripts discovered among the scrolls are nearly a thousand years closer to the time when the original books were written than are previously known manuscripts. They assist Old Testament textual criticism, especially by confirming the care with which the Hebrew text was transmitted. The scrolls and other material remains provide knowledge of a Jewish sect which existed in the time of Jesus, John the Baptist, and the early church. The background of the New Testament, therefore, is illuminated by these discoveries. The exact relationship of the Christian community to the Dead Sea community is still being studied.

VALUE OF ARCHAEOLOGY

If the purpose of biblical archaeology is not to prove the Bible, how can it help biblical study?

The literature which has been discovered, only part of which has been discussed previously, assists the Bible student in many ways.

Meanings of Words.—The documents make the Bible more intelligible by providing the previously unknown meaning of many words and phrases. For example, in Hosea 3:2 a word is used which does not occur elsewhere in the Old Testament. The word is *lethech,* and is used for a particular measure of barley. Since the word appeared nowhere else, Bible scholars felt that the text was in error and should be changed. But in two texts from Ugarit the word was used as it was in Hosea, to describe a unit of dry measure—although the size is not definitely stated.

A Hebrew word, *miqweh,* occurs in 1 Kings 10:28, in a description of Solomon's trading activity; but the meaning of the word has been unknown. The King James Version translates the word as "linen yarn": "And Solomon had horses brought out of Egypt, and linen yarn: the king's merchants received the linen yarn at a price." The American Standard Version has "droves": "And the horses which Solomon had were brought out of Egypt; and the king's merchants received them in droves, each drove at a price." Assyrian records indicate that the word must refer to a place, Kue, in Asia Minor. This is the translation of the Revised Standard Version, therefore: "And Solomon's import of horses was from Egypt and Kue, and the king's traders received them from Kue at a price."

A group of names appearing in 2 Kings 18:17; Jeremiah 39:13, and elsewhere were translated in the King James Version as personal names of individuals—Tartan, Rabshakeh, Rabsaris, and Rabmag. Assyrian inscriptions show that these words are actually titles of Assyrian officials. Tartan is the "commander-in-chief," Rabshakeh is probably the "field marshal," Rabsaris is perhaps the "chief eunuch," and Rabmag is apparently some other high official.

In Proverbs 26:23 two words are found which give some trouble, *kesef sigim.* The King James and the American Standard Versions translate this phrase as "silver dross." The King James Version says, "Burning lips and a wicked heart are like a potsherd covered with silver dross." The Ugaritic texts contain a word, *kesapsigim,*

which means "like glaze." No doubt this is the word found in Proverbs. The Revised Standard Version translates the verse, "Like the
glaze covering an earthen vessel are smooth lips with an evil heart."

Illustration of Practices.— Another important value lies in the
illustration of laws, customs, and religious practices mentioned in the
Bible. Many of these practices have been obscure.

In Deuteronomy 14:21, there is a command, " 'You shall not
boil a kid in its mother's milk' " (RSV). There is no apparent reason
for this law, and students have sought for some logical explanation
for it. In the Ras Shamra literature is a reference in a poem concerning cooking a kid in milk, and it is practically certain that this was a
Canaanite religious rite. The law in Deuteronomy is a forceful way of
telling the Israelites not to practice pagan religious rites.

In Genesis 16, Sarah gives her servant Hagar to Abraham in
order that she might bear him a son. Is this an isolated case, or is this
a common practice? In the Code of Hammurabi is evidence that this
was a common practice. It provides that a handmaid who has been
given by a wife to a husband and has borne him children may not be
sold. She may be made a slave. One of the documents (a marriage
contract) from Nuzi also says that if the wife is barren she must
provide another woman for her husband. When a child arrives as a
result of this union, however, the wife cannot drive out the child, as
Sarah drove out Ishmael (Gen. 21:10).

The tablets from Nuzi also shed some light on the theft of the
teraphim by Rachel when she and Leah fled with Jacob (Gen.
31:19). The tablets afford evidence that there was a connection
between the possession of the family gods and the right of inheri-
tance. Rachel wanted to be certain to secure for her husband the right
to inherit the property of Laban.

When Hezekiah was "sick unto death" with a boil, the prophet
Isaiah directed that he have a cake or lump of figs placed on the boil
(2 Kings 20:7; Isa. 38:21). The Ras Shamra tablets reveal the
significance of this direction by a record that lumps of figs were used
as poultices for horses. The medical use of figs was not an arbitrary
act of the prophet; it was a practice long recognized in the area.

CONTRIBUTION TO HISTORY OF BIBLE LANDS

Another major contribution of archaeology—from the study of
unwritten objects as well as written documents—is the knowledge of

the history of Palestine and its surrounding areas. Although the purpose of the Bible is not to give a comprehensive history of Palestine and her neighbors, a knowledge of the history of the Near East does aid in understanding the Bible. Until recently, however, there were many large gaps in the knowledge of the history of this area.

W. F. Albright declared that "there are few fields where the progress of discovery makes constant revision of handbooks and other aids to study more necessary than in Biblical research." He further stated that it has been in our generation "that the progress of research has made real synthesis possible." [6] In 1940, Albright published *From the Stone Age to Christianity*. Since then many books have been written utilizing recent archaeological discoveries in reconstructing the history of the Near East. As the history presented by the Bible is compared with the history presented by archaeology, several conclusions are reached as to the reliability of the Bible.

General Confirmation.—Archaeology confirms that the past presented in the Bible is *compatible* with the actual past known from archaeology. If the biblical materials were mere fiction, this fact would be exposed by items out of place. But the world of the Bible is the same world dug up by archaeologists.

Many ways in which archaeology gives general confirmation to the Bible are discussed by Millar Burrows in *What Mean These Stones?* He points out that the social customs uncovered in archaeological sources fit biblical stories of the patriarchal period. The topography of the narrative fits the findings of archaeology. The names of characters in the Bible, the names of non-Israelite gods, the general cultural and religious background, all accord with the knowledge gained from archaeological documents.

The general New Testament picture is also confirmed by archaeology. The book of Acts, for example, purports to show the developments within the Christian community from the death of Christ to Paul's imprisonment in Rome. In the last century some scholars were attracted to the theory that Acts was really written much later than the first century with second century ideas superimposed upon the narratives. Sir William Ramsay, however, demonstrated through his research in Asia Minor that the political, geographical, and historical atmosphere of Acts is that of the first century.

Specific Confirmation.—Although every detail of the biblical account has not been confirmed by archaeology, and some details have actually been called into question, many specific historical details have been confirmed.

In the cuneiform sources and lists of conquered cities made by Egyptian and Assyrian rulers there occur names of cities and countries which also occur in the early portions of the Old Testament. Burrows says, "Shiloh has been shown by excavation to have been unoccupied during the Late Bronze Age, occupied in the Early Iron Age, and destroyed at about 1050 B.C., exactly as required by the narratives of the Old Testament." He continues, "Gibeah was burned at about the time indicated by the account in Judges 20. Samaria was built at a time corresponding to the statement that Omri established it as the capital of the northern kingdom. The examples of such confirmation which might be given are almost innumerable." [7]

In a Babylonian record is an extraordinary confirmation of an account in 2 Kings. The statement in 2 Kings is that Jehoiachin was taken out of prison by Nebuchadnezzar's successor Evilmerodach, "and he did eat bread continually before him all the days of his life, and his allowance was a continual allowance given him of the king, a daily rate for every day, all the days of his life" (2 Kings 25:29–30). In Babylon tablets containing the names of people who were given regular allowances of grain and oil at the court of Babylon is the name of "Yaukin king of the land of Yahud." [8]

The New Testament is confirmed in many details. The accuracy of Luke 3:1 had been called into question. It states that Lysanias was tetrarch of Abilene when the word of God came to John in the wilderness. Lysanias died in 34 B.C., and scholars, therefore, concluded that Luke was wrong. An inscription, however, has been discovered which shows that there was another and later Lysanias of Abilene, although the exact dates of his reign are not known.

As indicated earlier, Ramsay concluded that the book of Acts was written in the first century because the general picture of that century recorded in Acts was confirmed by archaeology. In addition, there are specific items in Acts which are confirmed by archaeology. In Acts 18:12 Gallio is named as the proconsul of Achaia; an inscription not only confirms this fact but also gives the approximate date. Luke uses some special terms for Asian officials, "politarchs" at Thessalonica and "asiarchs" at Ephesus. The use is correct.

Care must be used in the employment of archaeological data to prove specific points in the Bible. Burrows states that "there are statements and stories in the Bible which cannot be reconciled with the course of events disclosed by archaeological discoveries."

Let the statement be emphasized again that the greatest contribution of archaeology is not the confirmation or nonconfirmation of specific points. Rather, it uncovers the evidence that enables scholars to reconstruct the conditions under which people lived in biblical times and to better understand biblical characters.

---

[1] G. W. Van Beek, "Archaeology," *The Interpreter's Dictionary of the Bible* (Nashville: Abingdon Press, 1962), I, 203.

[2] William Foxwell Albright, "The Rediscovery of the Biblical World," *The Westminster Historical Atlas to the Bible*, George Ernest Wright and Floyd Vivian Filson (eds.) (Philadelphia: The Westminster Press, 1945), p. 9.

[3] D. J. Wiseman, "Historical Records of Assyria and Babylonia," *Documents from Old Testament Times*, D. Winston Thomas (ed.) (New York: Harper and Row, 1961), p. 46.

[4] James B. Pritchard, *Archaeology and the Old Testament* (Princeton: Princeton University Press, 1958), p. 142.

[5] *Ibid.*, p. 206.

[6] Albright, *op. cit.*

[7] Millar Burrows, *What Mean These Stones?* (New Haven: A. S. O. R., 1941), p. 281.

[8] *Ibid.*, p. 282.

Explore It

Robert A. Baker

One of the great teachers of the Bible, J. B. Tidwell of Baylor University, often remarked to his classes that for over thirty years he had read an average of over a hundred books a year on the Bible; but that so far as mastering the Bible was concerned, he had "simply touched the hem of the garment." He was emphasizing that even with a lifetime of study—and, in his case, careful, intensive study—he could not claim a complete knowledge of the Bible.

The Importance of Study Methods

The wrong method of Bible study can result in a wrong interpretation of the Bible. Is it not a frightening thought, for example, to recall that the Pharisees of Jesus' day had probably done more study of the Scriptures and knew more about what they said than almost any other group in Jewish life? Despite all of this study, Jesus said to them, when they raised one of their test questions with him, that they did not know the Scriptures (Matt. 22:29). In their study, they had followed a method of gaining information that in some way had filtered out the truth; and they had missed it.

That is the reason for saying that after all the methods suggested in this book are exhausted, unless the Spirit of God illuminates our minds and our hearts, we still may be without understanding of the Bible. We have gained much information, but it will be empty knowledge.

Dr. Tidwell, mentioned above, urged that Bible students should approach God's Word with intelligence, with confidence, with reverence, with a ready assent to its teachings, with purpose to obey it, with a view to self-appropriation, with a spirit of rejoicing in it, with prayerfulness, with a view to finding Jesus in it, and with meditation.

Areas of Study

The Bible should be studied from many viewpoints. Challenging areas include biography, great events of the Bible, important periods in Bible history, great passages of the Bible, inspiring chapters, and individual books. Other approaches may be through meaningful themes, different kinds of writing in the Bible, and many other doctrinal and devotional emphases.

158

Methods of Study

The main thrust of this article, however, is concerned with methods for studying the Bible. Let us notice some basic methods that should be followed in the study of the Bible.

Words.—Whether you are studying an entire section, a single chapter, a paragraph within a chapter, or a single verse, you must begin your study with the words involved. You will never be able to interpret sentences or chapters without this step.

Every English word in the passage being studied should be understood clearly. A good dictionary is essential. In addition, different English versions of the Bible will be of great help.

After you understand the meaning of the words in a particular verse, it is well to make a list of the important words that are found.

For example, in Romans 12:1–2, some of the important words are "mercies," "present," "bodies," "living sacrifice," "holy," "acceptable," and "reasonable service." Look up these words in your Bible concordance, which lists the appearance of each word in the Bible. You can learn a great deal about a word's meaning by ascertaining how it is used elsewhere in the Bible.

Another question to ask is, How is this particular word used by the same writer elsewhere in the same book? Or, Is this the only time the word is used by this writer? How is this word used by another writer? Is it used extensively by this particular writer, or does he use it rarely? Is this the only occurrence of this particular word in the entire Bible? The answers to these questions will provide for you a store of important information about the meaning and use of the basic words of a particular verse.

As a matter of fact, many excellent Bible students make this a principal method of their study. They follow throughout the Bible important words such as "redemption," "praise," "worship."

Context.—After you have satisfied yourself that you have found all of the important meanings that can be secured from word study, you will then want to turn your attention to the setting of the particular verse you are studying. This setting or background is called the "context." "Context" refers to the material that goes along with the text. One of the greatest abuses of the Bible has been the practice of taking a Scripture verse out of its context. Perhaps you have heard someone say that you can prove anything by the Bible. You can do so only if you ignore the setting or context of a verse or a passage.

In determining the context of a verse, you must learn to relate it to the paragraph and chapter in which it is found. Is it the conclusion of a long argument? Is it the foundation verse which the writer unfolds during the next several paragraphs? Are there words in the verse that relate it to the materials that have gone before (such as "therefore" or "consequently")?

Study of the context is not enough. It is always wise to relate your verse to the large story of the Bible. Where is this verse found in the unfolding of God's revelation? How does it fit into the immediate circumstances of the Bible material surrounding it? It is a good thing to have the outlines of the books of the Bible near you so that you may see the place where this verse fits into the outline of the entire book and where the entire book fits into the larger story of the whole Bible.

Circumstances of writing.—You will now want to enlarge the area of your investigation. The circumstances under which a particular verse was written are usually of utmost significance.

Who wrote this particular verse—a prophet, a fisherman, an exile on Patmos? Under what circumstances was it written? Was the writer in jail, imprisoned in his own hired house, under the press of a busy ministry?

When was this verse written? Was it penned far back in primitive days when the full light of God's progressive revelation had not yet been comprehended?

At what time in the immediate experience of the writer was this verse recorded? Was it written in a time of great victory or of apparent defeat? Is it the last word we have from the pen of this writer? Is the tone of the writing what one would expect under the circumstances? If not, why is the tone different from what we expect?

How was this verse written? Did Paul dictate it to his secretary? Did Jeremiah give it as a replacement for a copy that had been burned? Did Luke collect the material after careful research?

Where was this verse written? Was Jeremiah in the midst of a stricken city? Was Paul writing from Ephesus, Corinth, or Rome? What was the purpose of the writing of this particular verse or book?

Perhaps you are tiring already from this variety of questions. This sort of curiosity, however, can help you dig out from the Bible many things that others will miss.

Historical references.—The Bible was written in the midst of history. You cannot possibly understand the Bible without understanding some history. When the Bible talks about centurions on the streets of Jerusalem or Roman soldiers in every city visited by Paul on his missionary journeys, you should always ask the question, How did they get there?

The Bible makes reference to historical people, such as Augustus Caesar and Pilate. It refers to customs and habits, to religious and political parties, and to a thousand other historical facts that can enrich greatly your understanding of the Bible. Your understanding will be greatly enriched by investigation of these historical references.

How could you possibly understand Acts 21:37–40, for instance, where Paul is pictured as being arrested by the Roman soldiers to prevent injury from a Jewish mob, had you not some understanding of the immediate history? In his defense, he spoke in both the Hebrew and the Greek, claimed Roman citizenship in a city noted for its Greek culture, and owed his allegiance to Jesus Christ. Such a variety in background in the life of a man demands some historical study on your part to explain it.

Relation to other teachings.—A good Bible student will never interpret a verse of Scripture without relating it to the revelation in the remainder of the Bible. "We must not study the Bible piecemeal. . . . Many false teachings have boasted biblical support by disregarding its [the Bible's] progressive revelation and its unity." [1]

Kind of writing.—It is important in our Bible study to recognize whether the particular verse being studied is a part of a poem, of Wisdom Literature, or of Jewish ceremonial law. Is it a parable, a riddle, or some other literary form used in writing?

It takes a great deal of study and training to know how to interpret each of these forms of writings. Many students have gone astray as they have tried to interpret a parable, for instance. They have tried to make every detail in the parable have some significance, when actually only one central truth must be emphasized. Similarly, songs and poems cannot be interpreted in the same way as one of the laws of Israel.

Leadership of the Spirit.—In all of this, as emphasized previously, there must be constant reliance upon the Holy Spirit of God to illumine and enlighten our hearts and our minds as we study the Word of God. [2]

[1] J. B. Weatherspoon, *The Book We Teach* (Nashville: Convention Press, 1934), p. 29. Used by permission.
[2] Robert A. Baker, *The Bible—The Book That Lives,* © 1965, The Sunday School Board of the SBC, pp. 55–58. This article was adapted by permission.

The Sermon on the Mount
An Outline of Matthew 5–7

Robert A. Dean

Jesus spoke these words to his disciples (5:1–2).

I. The joy of a disciple is based on the degree to which he shares a Christlike character (5:3–12).

   1. Joy belongs to the humble, because they belong to God (5:3).

   2. Joy belongs to the earnest, because they share God's comforting help (5:4).

   3. Joy belongs to men who are submissive to God, because all things belong to those who belong to God (5:5).

   4. Joy belongs to those who eagerly seek righteousness, because they shall be righteous (5:6).

   5. Joy belongs to the merciful, because they know God's merciful grace (5:7).

   6. Joy belongs to the pure in heart, because they know God best (5:8).

   7. Joy belongs to peacemakers, because all men recognize that they are God's children (5:9).

   8. Joy belongs to those persecuted for righteousness' sake, because they are most like their Lord (5:10–12).

II. A disciple can bear an influence for the Lord (5:13–16).

   1. A disciple is like salt because his influence can preserve a morally corrupt world (5:13).

   2. He is a light in the darkness reflecting the glory of Christ, who is the Light of the world (5:14–16).

III. A disciple's righteousness fulfils the moral demands of the Old Testament law (5:17–48).

   1. Not only will murder be judged, but also anger and scorn; therefore, a disciple should always take the initiative in seeking reconciliation (5:21–26).

   2. Not only will adultery be judged, but also lust; therefore, a disciple should practice the sternest kind of self-discipline (5:27–30).

Dr. Dean is editor of Adult Life and Work Lesson materials, Sunday School Department, Sunday School Board, Nashville, Tennessee.

3. Only under the most extreme circumstances should a man divorce his wife, for marriage should be a lifetime relationship (5:31–32).

4. Using oaths to establish the truth of what you say should be unnecessary for men of absolute honesty (5:33–37).

5. Instead of a spirit of revenge, a disciple should practice forbearance and generosity (5:38–42).

6. Instead of hating his enemies, a disciple should seek to do good to his enemies, for this is the way God deals with all of us (5:43–48).

IV. A disciple should do good in order to please God, not men (6:1–18).

1. He should give to help others, but he should not give so as to call attention to his generosity (6:1–4).

2. He should pray in trust to God his Heavenly Father, but he should never pray in order to be seen by others (6:5–15).

3. He should practice self-denial, but he should try to avoid calling the attention of others to his dedication (6:16–18).

V. A disciple should examine his attitude toward material things (6:19–34).

1. He should focus his attention on values that are eternal and avoid building his life on transient things (6:19–21).

2. He should practice single-hearted commitment to God, because no man can serve more than one master (6:22–24).

3. He should distinguish between making a living and living a life (6:25).

4. He should realize that anxiety about material things never accomplished any good (6:26–27).

5. Anxiety should be replaced by trust in God (6:28–30).

6. When a disciple puts first things first, other things take care of themselves (6:31–33).

7. A man of faith tries to live only one day at a time (6:34).

VI. A disciple should be careful about his relationships with others (7:1–12).

1. No man has the right to set himself up as God and judge others, because all of us have our faults (7:1–5).

2. On the other hand, neither should we enter into any relationship that will compromise our commitment to the Lord we serve (7:6).

3. Such living requires the strength and guidance that comes from continuing prayer to God our Father (7:7–11).
4. A disciple should do that good toward others that he wants others to do toward him (7:12).

VII. A disciple should put his discipleship to the test (7:13–27).
1. He should examine his life to see if he is walking in the way of Christ, not in the way of the crowd (7:13–14).
2. He should beware the deception of false prophets who have many outward marks of true prophets but whose false motives are revealed in the ultimate outcome of their work (7:15–20).
3. The judgment of God is not based on what we profess to be but on our knowledge of Christ revealed in a life of obedience to the will of God (7:21–23).
4. A person has not really heard the word of the Lord until he does what the Lord says to do (7:24–27).

Conclusion: The people were astonished at the authority with which Jesus spoke these words (7:28–29).

A Study Outline of Romans
Robert A. Dean

Introduction: Paul sent greetings to the Roman church and set forth his theme—the righteousness of God (1:1–17).

I. God is righteous in condemning sinners because all have sinned (1:18 to 3:20).
  1. The wrath of God is being revealed against the many dark sins of the Gentiles (1:18–32).
    (1) They turned their backs on God (1:18–21).
    (2) They turned to idolatry (1:22–25).
    (3) They practiced immoral perversions (1:26–27).
    (4) They reaped social chaos (1:28–32).
  2. The Jews, who are so quick to judge the sins of others, are also under the judgment of God (2:1 to 3:20).
    (1) God's judgment is inescapable and impartial (2:1–11).
    (2) God will judge men not according to who they are, but according to what they have done (2:12–29).
    (3) The Jews were intrusted with the laws of God, but they stand condemned by their Scriptures, which clearly teach that all have sinned (3:1–20).

II. God is righteous in justifying sinners through faith in Christ (3:21 to 5:21).
  1. The cross is God's supreme redemptive act, showing God to be just in justifying sinners (3:21–31).
  2. Sinners are justified through faith in Christ, not through the works of the law (4:1–25).
    (1) Old Testament heroes like Abraham and David were justified by faith (4:1–13).
    (2) Abraham's faith in God's power to give Sarah the child of promise is like a Christian's faith in God's power that raised up Jesus from the dead (4:14–25).
  3. Joyful assurance is the result of being justified through faith (5:1–11).
    (1) Peace with God leads to joy, even in trials (5:1–4).
    (2) Hope is based on the inner experience of the Spirit and confirmed by the love of God seen in the death of Christ (5:5–8).

       (3) Assurance of final salvation grows out of being reconciled to God now (5:9–11).

    4. Christ thus offers life to a race under the tyranny of sin and death (5:12–21).

III. God is righteous in producing a new life for those in Christ (6:1 to 8:39).

    1. Life in Christ means a union with Christ that is incompatible with a continued life of sin (6:1 to 7:6).

       (1) A believer in Christ has been joined with Christ in a death to self and sin (6:1–11).

       (2) Having been liberated from slavery to sin, a Christian should not return to its tyranny (6:12 to 7:6).

    2. Christ offers freedom from the hopeless and helpless plight of those who strive in their own strength to meet the demands of the law (7:7–25).

       (1) Sin stirs up evil desires and thus distorts the good purpose of the law (7:7–13).

       (2) When men trust in their own strength, they are morally incapable of breaking sin's hold over them (7:14–24).

       (3) Only Christ can do that (7:25).

    3. The indwelling presence of God's Spirit in a believer makes possible a new life (8:1–27).

       (1) The Spirit of Christ gives a believer new interests and new power to live for God (8:1–11).

       (2) A Christian, therefore, should live after the Spirit, not after the flesh (8:12–14).

       (3) Those who are led by the Spirit are God's sons, who share God's strength in present suffering and look with hope toward final redemption (8:15–25).

       (4) The Spirit even teaches us to pray (8:26–27).

    4. A believer can face life unafraid because of God's grace (8:28–39).

       (1) God's good purpose for his people is that they be conformed to the image of Christ (8:28–30).

       (2) No one can condemn but God, and God has chosen to be the Saviour of men (8:31–34).

       (3) Nothing, therefore, can separate us from God's love for us (8:35–39).

IV. God is righteous in his dealings with both Jews and Gentiles (9:1 to 11:36).
   1. God is free to deal with men as he chooses (9:1–29).
      (1) Paul was deeply concerned over Israel's lost plight (9:1–5).
      (2) Some said that God's covenant with Israel obligated God to save Israel, but Paul said that God is sovereign and free (9:6–18).
      (3) If God chose to do so, he could fashion men for destruction, but God has chosen to offer mercy to sinners (9:19–29).
   2. Men are lost because they have rejected God's merciful call (9:30 to 10:21).
      (1) How can Israel's lostness be accounted for? (9:30–33).
      (2) Israel rejected God's way of faith-righteousness and clung to her own way of works-righteousness (10:1–13).
      (3) Israel had had every opportunity to hear and to heed the gospel, but she had rejected God's call (10:14–21).
   3. God deals with men in such a way as to lead as many as possible to salvation (11:1–36).
      (1) Israel's loss was not complete; God's true people have always been a remnant (11:1–12).
      (2) God is still at work among both Jews and Gentiles; therefore, Gentiles should shun pride, and Jews should take hope (11:13–24).
      (3) God's ultimate purpose is to bestow mercy on all who will respond (11:25–36).
 V. God is righteous in guiding believers to lead a life of dedication and love (12:1 to 15:13).
   1. God's grace should inspire complete dedication to godly living (12:1–2).
   2. Christians should live according to the law of Christlike love (12:3–21).
      (1) They should practice this love toward brothers in Christ (12:3–13).
      (2) They should also practice love toward their enemies (12:14–21).

3. Critical times demand the best of God's people (13:1–14).
   (1) Christians owe obedience to the government (13:1–7).
   (2) They owe love to their fellowmen (13:8–10).
   (3) They owe holy living to God (13:11–14).
4. Christians have a special obligation to practice the law of
   love in their dealings with one another (14:1 to 15:13).
   (1) No believer should judge his brother because all will
       be judged by Christ (14:1–12).
   (2) Instead of judging our brother, we should love him by
       not doing anything that might harm him (14:13–23).
   (3) This principle of Christlike love applies even whether
       our brothers be Jews or Gentiles (15:1–13).

Conclusion: Paul explained his personal plans (15:14–33) and sent
his personal greetings to friends in the Roman church (16:1–27).

A Book Study of Ephesians
Charles Treadway

INTRODUCTION

Author: Paul, probably, though some say not—because of vocabulary and style. There are some who say Timothy or Onesimus or some other wrote it and Paul signed it.

Date: A.D. 60–63—probably from Rome during Paul's first imprisonment. ". . . a prisoner for the Lord" (Eph. 4:1, RSV).

Readers: Probably written to a group of churches rather than just the Ephesian church. Composed for Christian residents of the Roman province of Asia Minor—a circular letter. Four reasons:

1. Tychicus (Eph. 6:21–22 and Col. 4:7–8, reference made to him as going on general mission of instruction, as a bearer of letters).
2. No *specific* problem mentioned in the book as was mentioned in Colossians. The book is general.
3. Evidence that many of the readers not acquainted with Paul—he had spent much of his time in Ephesus.
4. Term "in Ephesus" not found in three of best and oldest manuscripts.

Destination: Ephesus, the commercial and political capital of Roman province of Asia Minor. Temple of Diana here—one of seven wonders of the world—425 feet long, 220 feet wide, of shining marble, supported by 127 columns, each 60 feet in height, and each a gift of a king—220 years in construction. Inside the building was image of the goddess, Diana, said to have fallen from the heavens.

Behind the shrine, kings and nations had stored their wealth in the treasury. Another building located here was the great theater, largest in the Hellenic world, held 24,500 spectators —mob had attempted to drag Paul here.

Purpose: Why was it written? To establish the readers in their Christian faith; to guard them against the danger of forgetting as Jews and Gentiles their uniting in the body of Christ; to

Dr. Treadway is a consultant, Pastoral Ministries section, Church Administration Department, the Sunday School Board, Nashville, Tennessee.

guard them against drifting back into old practices and ways
of life.

Content: Against backdrop of these memories, and in the atmosphere of Roman imprisonment, Paul emphasized two themes.
They are:

1. The Grace of God (1:1 to 3:21). (To the church.)
2. The Christian Life (4:1 to 6:24). (Exhortation to life
   worthy of that grace, for truth must be expressed in
   life.)

Key word: Unity

Unity of Jews and Gentiles in Christ, unity of church,
unity of members.

Epistle divided into two great sections of three chapters each:

1. Doctrinal—Christian faith (chaps. 1, 2, and 3).
   Sets forth the grace of God (what God has done for us).
2. Practical—Christian life (chaps. 4, 5, and 6).
   This section is composed of exhortations to recipients
   of this grace (what God expects of us), giving us "a
   blueprint of the Christian life."

OUTLINE: Doctrinal Section: What God has done for us
                     (chaps. 1–3)

Salutation: (1:1–2)

  I. God's Eternal Purpose in Christ (1:3–14)
    1. Blessings of God's people (1:3–6)
      (1) Their nature—"spiritual" (1:3)
      (2) Basis on which blessings are bestowed (1:4–6)
    2. Description of these blessings (1:7–14)
      (1) Redemption and forgiveness (1:7)
      (2) Wisdom and insight (1:8–10)
      (3) A heavenly inheritance (1:11–12)
      (4) Gift of the Holy Spirit (1:13–14)
 II. Petition for Understanding of God's Purpose and Power
     (1:15–23)
    1. Thanksgiving for faith and love (1:15*a*)
    2. Continued prayer in their behalf: "That ye may know"
       (1:16–23):
      (1) The hope inspired by the call of God (1:16–17)
      (2) How precious is the church to God (1:18)
      (3) The greatness of the power of God (1:19–23)

  III. Spiritual Resurrection of Men in Union with Christ (2:1–10)
      1. Man's plight—needs to be saved (2:1–3)
      2. God's gift—way of salvation (2:4–9)
      3. Good works—purpose and expression of salvation (2:10)
  IV. The Unification (reconciliation) of Jew and Gentile in Christ
      (2:11–22)
      1. Their former state of spiritual death and present state
        (2:11–13*a*)
      2. What Christ has done through the cross (2:13*b*–18)
      3. Unity of believers in Christ (2:19–22)
   V. Paul's Interpretation of Grace (3:1–21)
      1. The mystery of the gospel (3:1–9)
      2. God's plan for the ages (3:10–13)
      3. Prayer for Christians in the light of this glorious truth
        (3:14–19)
      4. Doxology growing out of things prayed for (3:20–21)
Practical Section: Spirit and Duties of Christians (4:1 to 6:24)
  VI. Christian Unity—Growing in Grace (4:1–16)
     Christ: God's instrument for reconciling the world unto him-
       self.
     Church: As Christ's body, all Christians are the instruments
       God has chosen to achieve this reconciliation.
     God's aim: "a sacred oneness"—"a new togetherness"—with
       Christ supplying the one center around whom and in whom
       all men can be gathered.
      1. Virtues that contribute to unity (4:1–3)
        (1) Humility
        (2) Gentleness
        (3) Long-suffering
        (4) Love
        (5) Peace
      2. Foundations of Christian unity and growth (4:4–6)
        (1) One body
        (2) One spirit
        (3) One hope
        (4) One Lord
        (5) One faith
        (6) One baptism
        (7) One God and Father

   3. Functions of growing Christians in the church (4:7–16)
      (1) For the perfecting of the saints
      (2) Building up the body of Christ
      (3) Securing unity and maturity of the church
VII. The Challenge of Christian Morality (4:17 to 5:21)
   1. The Gentile way (4:17–19)
      (1) Vanity (v. 17)—concerned with empty things
      (2) Blindness (v. 18)—darkened mind
      (3) Past feeling (v. 19)—petrified
      (4) Lasciviousness (v. 19)—more beast than man
      (5) Greediness (v. 19)—unlawful desire
   2. The Christian way (4:20–24)
      (1) Truth only in Christ (v. 21)
      (2) Old man replaced with new man (vv. 22–24)
      (3) Way of renewal (v. 23)
   3. Challenge to application of new life (4:25 to 5:21)
      (1) Honesty must replace dishonesty (4:25)
      (2) Controlled temper must replace hate (4:26–27)
      (3) Work must replace stealing (4:28)
      (4) Good speech must replace corrupt speech (4:29)
      (5) Must be kind and walk in love (4:30 to 5:5)
      (6) Must walk in light and wisdom (5:6–21)
          a. Be careful how you live
          b. Make best use of your time and opportunities
          c. Demonstrate the Christian way of life
VIII. A Living Fellowship—Being Christian in the Home (5:22 to 6:9)
   Unity: key to relationships of Christians in the church
   Purity: demand in society
   Love: comprehensive word in the Christian home
   1. Duty of wife to husband (5:22–24)
      Recognition of husband's headship in home as Christ is head in the church.
   2. Duty of husband to wife (5:25–33)
      (1) Sacrificial love (v. 25)
      (2) Purifying love (v. 26)
      (3) A caring love (vv. 28–29)
      (4) An unbreakable love (vv. 30–31)
      (5) A relationship "in the Lord" (vv. 32–33)

3. Duty of child to parents (6:1–3)
   "Keep on obeying," the first or primary commandment with promise
4. Duty of parent to child (6:4)
   The lot of child in Rome was tragic. Paul pleaded for child to be allowed to become a real person.
5. Remember that Christ is Lord (6:5–9)
   (1) God, no respecter of persons
   (2) Christianity, a continual conflict
IX. Christians and Conflict (6:10–24)
   1. The Christian's ally—God (6:10–11a)
   2. His enemy—Satan (6:11b–12)
   3. His equipment (6:13–20)
      (1) Girdle—truth (6:14a)
      (2) Breastplate—righteousness (6:14b)
      (3) Sandals—readiness (6:15)
      (4) Shield—faith (6:16)
      (5) Helmet—salvation (6:17a)
      (6) Sword—God's Word (6:17b)
   4. Prayer, an additional source of strength (6:18–20)
   5. Conclusion (6:21–24)
      (1) Personal matters (6:21–22)
      (2) Benediction (6:23–24)

SUGGESTED READING

Barclay, William. *The Letters to the Galatians and Ephesians*. Philadelphia: The Westminster Press, 1958.

Barth, Marcus. *Broken Wall*. Valley Forge: The Judson Press, 1959.

Bruce, F. F. *Epistle to the Ephesians*. Westwood, New Jersey: Fleming H. Revell Company, 1961.

Carver, W. O. *The Glory of God in the Christian Calling*. Nashville: Broadman Press, 1949.

Good News for Modern Man: Today's English Version. New York: American Bible Society, 1966.

Jordan, Clarence L. *The Cotton Patch Version of Paul's Epistles*. New York: Association Press, 1968.

Kelly, Balmer H. (ed.). *The Layman's Bible Commentary*. Richmond: John Knox Press, XXII, 1959.

Mackay, John. *God's Order*. New York: The Macmillan Company, 1953.

Moody, Dale. *Christ and the Church*. Grand Rapids: William B. Eerdmans Publishing Company, 1963.

Mullins, E. Y. *Studies in Ephesians*. Nashville: Convention Press, 1935.

Summers, Ray. *Ephesians: Pattern for Christian Living*. Nashville: Broadman Press, 1960.

Vaughan, Curtis W. *The Letter to the Ephesians*. Nashville: Convention Press, 1963.

Suggested Audiovisual Materials

Chapter 1

FILMSTRIPS: *The Book of Books,* 44 frames, color, recording; *Shimabuku,* 49 frames, color, recording

Chapter 2

FILMSTRIPS: *The Bible Comes to America,* 40 frames, color, recording; *The Bible, a Book for Everyone,* 48 frames, color, recording; *Bible Scrolls,* 60 frames, color, recording; *Getting the Most Out of Your Bible,* 47 frames, color, recording

MOTION PICTURES: *Making of the English Bible,* 35 minutes; *The Dead Sea Scrolls,* 14 minutes, color

Chapter 3

FILMSTRIPS: *A Survey of the Bible,* 40 frames, color, recording; "Survey of the Scriptures" (set of 10 filmstrips, color, recording)—*The Book of Books,* 44 frames; *The Pentateuch,* 42 frames; *The Rise of the Hebrew Nation,* 42 frames; *The Decline of the Hebrew Nation,* 42 frames; *Books of Poetry,* 42 frames; *The Prophetical Books,* 49 frames; *Between the Testaments,* 38 frames; *The Four Gospels,* 37 frames; *The Book of Acts,* 41 frames; *Romans to Revelation,* 45 frames; "Great Personalities of the Bible" (set of 6 filmstrips, color, manuals, 3 recordings with 2 separate and complete stories on each filmstrip)—*Abraham,* 42 frames and *Jacob,* 27 frames; *Joseph,* 35 frames and *Moses,* 35 frames; *David,* 38 frames and *Solomon,* 35 frames; *The Life of Jesus: His Birth and Boyhood,* 39 frames and *The Life of Jesus: The Beginning of His Ministry,* 24 frames; *The Life of Jesus: The Closing Ministry,* 21 frames and *The Life of Jesus: His Suffering and Death,* 37 frames; *Peter,* 30 frames and *Paul,* 44 frames

Chapter 4

FILMSTRIPS: "Bible Backgrounds, Part I" (set of 4 filmstrips, color, recordings)—*The Temples of the Pharaohs,* 41 frames; *Tyre, the City That Vanished,* 44 frames; *Petra, the Fortress of Esau,* 50 frames; *Babylon, the Glory of Kingdoms,* 26 frames; "Bible Backgrounds, Part II" (set of 4 filmstrips, color, recordings)—*The Tombs of the Pharaohs,* 39 frames; *The Wisdom of Egypt,* 42 frames; *Byblos, Gateway to the Past,* 33 frames; *The Grandeur of Rome,* 53 frames; "Bible Backgrounds, Part III" (set of 4 filmstrips, color, recordings)—*Baalbek, Glory of This World,* 42 frames; *Egypt and the Bible,* 43 frames; *Baalbek, Gateway to Palestine,* 33 frames; *The Glory of Greece,* 40 frames; "Bible Backgrounds, Part IV" (set of 4 filmstrips, color, recordings)—*Greek Gods and the Gospel,* 40 frames; *Palmyra, Ancient Caravan City,* 41 frames; *Jordan, Land of Promise,* 40 frames; *Pompeii, a Portrait of Roman Life,* 47 frames; "The Covenant God and His Covenant People" (set of 4 filmstrips, color, recordings)—*God's Covenant with Israel,* 40 frames; *God Keeps Covenant with His People,* 42 frames; *God's Covenant Fulfilled in Jesus Christ,* 43 frames; *The Early Church— God's New Covenant People,* 40 frames

Chapter 5

FILMSTRIP: *Getting the Most Out of Your Bible,* 47 frames, color, recording

A filmstrip, *How to Study the Bible,* has been released in conjunction with this book. It is suitable for use in preview of this volume, in connection with the class sessions, or as review after the book is studied. The filmstrip, manual, and recording are available at Baptist Book Stores.

Personal Learning Activities

Chapter 1

    1. List the four contexts in which Bible study is conducted today.

    2. List the three incentives for Bible study discussed in this chapter.

    3. List in your own words the personal values that can come to you through Bible study.

Chapter 2

    4. The collection of the Hebrew Bible was completed in _____.

    5. The selection of the New Testament books was finally accepted by Easter, _____.

    6. The Greek translation of the Old Testament is called the _____.

    7. List name, date, and sponsors of three major English translations of the Bible.

    8. List and describe five important tools for Bible study.

    9. List qualifications for Bible study.

Chapter 3

    10. List and give an illustration to show what the author meant by three principles of biblical interpretation.

    11. What guidance for private Bible study follows chapter 3 of this book? Which one will you undertake on your own?

Chapter 4

    12. List the guidelines for Bible study given in this chapter and give an example of each type of study.

    13. Read one day's assignment from chart on page 106 and prepare a notebook sheet on your reading. Use these headings:

        Reference
        Outstanding personalities
        Central themes
        Quotations
        Questions for further study

14. List three ways of studying the Bible by central themes as outlined by Ashcraft.

15. Answer these questions with information from the Brooks article on pages 113–17.

    (1) The key word of the Old Testament is _____.

    (2) There are two basic types of above: _____ and _____.

    (3) List the Old Testament words for love: _____; _____; _____; _____; _____; _____.

    (4) Define the following Greek words for love:

        philia _____

        storge _____

        philadelphia _____

        philanthropia _____

        agapē _____

Chapter 5

16. List five questions concerning Bible study which this book was developed to answer.

17. Fill in blanks in statements below with information from chapter five.

    (1) The law set forth in the Old Testament is essentially a _____ and _____ message.

    (2) The Bible is addressed to the _____ of God.

    (3) The fact that the Bible can be understood by Christians was affirmed during the _____.

    (4) In order to make wise personal decisions, a Christian needs: (list four qualities which Dr. Binkley suggests).

18. List the seven passages which are suggested for intensive study. Underline those for which study guides are included in this book.

19. How many hours per week does Dr. Binkley recommend one should spend in intensive Bible study in addition to Sunday School?

20. List at least five Bible study guides in this book which you plan to use in your own private Bible study.